Unwrapping Racism

Dealing with Differences

Chuck Grose

Series in Social Equality and Justice

VERNON PRESS

www.vernonpress.com

In the Americas:
Vernon Press
1000 N West Street, Suite 1200
Wilmington, Delaware, 19801
United States

In the rest of the world:
Vernon Press
C/Sancti Espiritu 17,
Malaga, 29006
Spain

Series in Social Equality and Justice

Library of Congress Control Number: 2023937188

ISBN: 978-1-64889-679-8

Table of Contents

Acknowledgments

For me, it took many communities to raise this author and to write "Unwrapping Racism."

Current Family members. Sons Justus, Pete, Mark, Paul, Daniel, daughters Mary Ruth, Lenoska, Johnnie, Jane, and my wife, Trish, recognize that my passionate pursuit of racial issues can nurture a more equitable world. Nephews and nieces, near and far, respect my risk-taking and activism as embodied in my book.

Dean, professor and support for teaching opportunities. Dean Walter Muelder ventilated the profound issues of life and articulated the Good News for individuals and the structures of society. The Dean introduced me and other students to Martin Luther King, Jr. and Howard Thurman at Boston University School of Theology. King elucidated social ethics and the study of God in action in Muelder's classes as a PhD candidate. Howard Thurman, University Chaplain, lived and preached a mystical inner joy. He added depth to life and became the inspiration for the substance and style of my writing.

Colleagues and friends. No friends were better supporters of my justice advocacy than Margaret Preska, Don and Pat Renner, and Patty Sho's family in Belize.

Initiator. Dennis Crow, friend and colleague, motivated me to add a section on journaling to my book.

Nudger. Lee H. Hamilton, an international educator and national administrative political leader, coached me to be the best of what I have learned.

Administrators. At Huston-Tillotson College, Austin, Texas, my administrators trusted me with essential priorities and leadership roles. Women leaders, in particular, taught me to be a servant leader.

Encouragers. Faye Kanne, Tim McGlennen and Cindy Saufferer keep raising our level of friendship to a higher standard and inspire my book to excel.

Model. Doug Wingeier was a role model, scholar, author, activist and friend who stimulated the individual and institutional racial actions that bring my book to everyday life.

Healers. Bretnie Eschenbach, Maureen Lunde, Rochelle Bauman and Karin Ryan elicit a different type of sense to my senses. Granddaughter Bretnie's deeply caring and technological expertise lift my life in unanticipated ways. Technical expert Maureen Lunde relieves stress and restores energy for my book as an advisor. Rochelle Bauman needs my needy muscles while guiding my body therapy. Karin Ryan addresses my emotional issues and highlights empathy and decision-making.

Editors. Argiris Legatos, Blanca Caro, Kimberly Rude and marketing director Javier Rodriguez, like no one else, understand the imminent need for my defining racial messages to be heard and implemented.

Church members. These churches of color nourished my spirit with reciprocity and generosity: Wesley United Methodist Church, Austin, Texas, Hmong Community United Methodist Church, St. Paul, Minnesota, Bad River United Methodist Church, Odanah, Wisconsin, and Barker Road Methodist Church, Singapore. Mayflower UCC, Minneapolis continues my zest for unequivocal racial redemption.

Introducing Unwrapping Racism: Dealing with Differences

Strategic to today's topsy-turvy democracy is why skin color still enflames pain and violence. We, and our groups, can change that racial hierarchy in the U. S. and beyond (Grose 2023). You, the reader, empower the hero of your racial actions (Hemendez, 8 Nov, 2022).

Author's Experiences and Overall Perspectives on Race

My in-depth, powerful experiences with people of color is the lifelong source of my passion for all racial encounters. This passion for racial justice began more as a journey in which I was trying to understand myself in terms of the whole world. In my gut, I intentionally sought face-to-face interactions with persons of different racial backgrounds. It meant I would learn from them in their own communities!

A telegram came to me in Singapore from a Black college president in Austin, Texas. He recruited me to teach sociology at Huston-Tillotson College, a historically-Black college. I was warmly received by its students, faculty and staff; it was challenging for me as their only white colleague. That entire experience continues to motivate my passion, understanding and focus on race relations.

Out of classroom experiences included participation in civil rights marches, demonstrations against the Ku Klux Klan, leading in Austin's City Council meetings with Black community members, serving as a community organizer in Black communities, and lecturing with Volunteers in Service to America (VISTA). Also fascinating for me was to live in a Black community and lead in a Black church for 11 years.

Hired by other groups of color, I co-led a Hmong institution, served as an American Indian community worker, and taught in the only two colleges of the diverse country Belize, Central America.

Picture in your mind my many experiences associated with teaching in historically-white institutions like Olivet College in Michigan, and Minnesota State University, Mankato, Minnesota. Seated in a circle, the racially diverse student groups engaged each other and me while learning by discussion. Most of the students of color respected how I dealt with racial issues and were empowered by my leadership.

Many of us are unclear about how we deal with human differences. Some see differences as only a way to seek common understanding – not as ends in themselves. Others view racial differences as relationships that need minimizing or hiding for whatever reason or no reason.

Consider my approach. Differences are not the problem. Rather it is how our feelings and thoughts address social differences. That is challenging, complex and changing.

Each chapter in this book is filled with numerous paragraphs which show how the reader may vitally act on race. All the designed projects, exercises and some of the questions also may be utilized with other issues of the book. The final chapter exclusively approaches how to make a difference with our racial conundrum.

Our Background to Multi-Racial Excellence

You, I, and everyone desire to achieve the utmost in our lives, and for our offspring. One profound approach to this goal is to equip ourselves for that to happen. So we anticipate, prepare, plan, and act upon our goals that dynamically include viable racial relationships. This contextual background inspires others to join us in exploring that racial part of our goals, including racial engagements.

You and I bring ourselves to the vibrant and volatile daily experiences with race. Our questions, biases, memories, lingering thoughts, and personal "baggage" of awkward scripts present the context for our encounters with racial relationships. There is singular and plural power in that background.

And, we pull up the societal frameworks for our present-day racial context. These fundamental structures include where and when we were born, family life, friendship patterns, political systems, spiritual frames of reference, educational environment, and media connections.

Journaling

Neurological Journaling

Basically, the neurons of the brain initiate the optic nerve through the neurological pathways to connect with the hand. Simplified, this process illuminates thinking to create new insights and understanding throughout the body systems. That interplay within the neurological process brings meaning to what we call journaling (Ryan, Oct. 25, 2022).

An in depth, scholarly description of this journaling is presented by Dr. Karin Ryan.

Journaling has neurobiological benefits, including increased neuroplasticity, allowing your brain to grow and adjust. When you write, you are activating many parts of your brain, including your frontal lobe for interpreting words and language, your occipital lobe as you see your writing, and your motor cortex as you move your arm and hand (Ryan, Nov. 17, 2022).

Psychological Responses with Journaling

Some of our awesome moments, creative ideas, and deep feelings bubble up while journaling.

It permeates our intellectual juices with newly discovered inspirational ideas.

It awakens our sluggish feelings that stimulate tender, heartfelt experiences.

When both head and heart resonate, we may touch the keys of harmonious blending.

All these beautiful experiences are similar to hearing those all-encompassing musical sounds while sitting inside an orchestra.

Our individual writing insights may be less glorious, and may only clarify an anticipated word or expression.

Often our journaling thoughts seem routine, stale, stuck, trite, or we may "call timeout."

And our feelings may be shallow, dull, lacking empathy or distracted by our dominating thoughts.

They may become like the string instrument that strikes a shrill note.

Or we may dispel our feelings, and launch a few questions. Our journaling may grow through questions we dismiss, or expedite.

Kinds of Journaling

In essence, our journaling may be eclectic, multi-directional, probing, and it uses critical thinking.

Eclectic journaling accepts the greatest variety of persons and circumstances and sees them in their unique and disjointed experiences. For instance, persons with disadvantaged backgrounds and the privileged elites are recognized in their less powerful and more powerful characteristics.

Multi-directional journaling has the ability to imagine the impact of social forces on individual lives, and include empathy. For example, this kind of writing goes beyond either/or thinking and looks for multiple approaches to persons frequently unnoticed or hidden, or obscured from our vision.

<u>Probing</u> journaling investigates a layered background of what is behind issues. Thoughts, feelings, change and connections to each day's experience are addressed. For example, what are our own decision-making behaviors around the racial hierarchy?

<u>Critical thinking</u> journaling weighs various viewpoints by way of comparing and/or contrasting an issue or issues. Through skepticism, curiosity and doubt, this thought process questions an argument or conclusion. For instance, are there alternative views about race that are based on new evidence or heartfelt feelings?

Other journaling initiatives by the reader also are encouraged. For example, the reader is challenged to journal with any questions not designated in my book's list. All phases of journaling are appropriate for group experience and/or individual opportunities. If the journaling needs to be read by others, they may expect a formal, grammatical approach. Confidentiality may be needed. Otherwise, a free-flowing style without commas and periods will suffice.

Journaling Action

Effective and genuine journaling may occur in a single sentence or phrase, or within a paragraph. Consequently, it may reflect only one type of journaling. For greater insight and development, the reader can plan to adopt all the above kinds of journaling by the time of completing the book.

Works Cited

Grose, Chuck. Introductory statement. 16 Feb, 2023.

Hemendez, Alicia. MSNBC election show, adaptation of her word "hero," 8 Nov, 2022.

Ryan, Karin. Consultation. Eden Prairie, Minnesota, 25 Oct and 17 Nov, 2022.

Chapter 1

Thinking and Feeling about Differences as a Guide for Race Relations

"What inspires us is the things that we didn't expect, or the people who are not like us, or the ideas or sounds we've never heard before" (Chude-Sokei 60).

Contemplate your encounters with differences

We benefit from the "majority of this planet who still craves more information and bursts with ideas and imagination." Let it be true for us. Your values and identity become the context from which you newly grapple with the power of race. In this chapter, we are engaging the dynamic circumstances that make race so real.

You will be re-introduced to yourself throughout this chapter. This means telling your own story of dealing with individual, racial and cultural differences. Your adventure of self-disclosure will be revealed by engaging in open-ended emotional and rational exercises.

What often catches our attention are negative thoughts and actions associated with human difference. How frequently do we assume that our differences are problems. For example, "It's not that I don't like them, it is just that they are different." We might ask what is the real meaning of this expression? Or as a friend said, "We will never get rid of our social differences. We can work on them and eventually try to eliminate some. Then we can gain some unity." We might ponder why unity or similarity should be the typically accepted conclusion. Resolution is not always understood as agreement or reaching a common goal. Rather what is important may be the ways we work on being together with differences.

An essential assumption drawn from my cross-cultural and international experiences is that we can be challenged by our differences and be intentional in promoting their value. Race, ethnicity, gender, religion, politics, language and sexual orientation need not lead to conflict, separation and violence. In this book, we explore how to ponder our racial differences, learn from their unusual qualities, affirm positive actions with other persons and groups, and explore how our culture can get rid of race and its hierarchy.

Exercise on Values Clarification Connected to Race

advancement	aesthetics	affiliation	creative expression	creativity
diversity	education	environment	family	friendships	fun and humor
help others	help society	honesty and integrity	group and team	fair earnings
independence	influence people	intellectual status		job security
knowledge	location	makes decisions	moral fulfillment	personal safety
power and authority	practicality	physical challenge	profit, gain	public contact
recognition	security	spirituality	stability	status	tradition

Rank about ten of the values, and journal which ones you consider more important.

Questions

1. What lies behind your prioritizing?

2. How do you perceive those ten ranked values relating to race?

Racism survives due to being enmeshed in the dynamics and relationships that form our society. That means a coordinated exclusion and segregation, inequality, and the degradation of labor (Bouie SR7).

An equalization of power must involve "a revolution of values" that would "look uneasily on the glaring contrast of poverty and wealth" and see that "an edifice which produces beggars needs restructuring," declared Dr. Martin Luther King, Jr. "Inequality is not only a moral issue but it is also intelligent." Clinging to archaic thinking degrades and wastes human life (Bouie SR7).

Questions and Journaling

1. How do you think there can be a revolution of values? How do you picture that being done?

2. Briefly write how you would identify some of those revolutionary values.

3. How might life be different because of restructuring those values? You could explore values in relation to institutions, informal culture and otherwise.

4. How might the revolution be empowered and made accountable?

Stark, deep, dismissive and distracting are some of our discussions about social differences.

"Don't believe everything you think" is a bumper sticker that can stimulate varied approaches to differences and racism. Talk with a person about what this bumper sticker might mean.

Questions

1. How would you describe what is meant by social differences?

2. Try to identify how the idea on the bumper sticker can be applied to both positive and negative racial situations.

Distinctive to any discussion of race is skin color. And that assumes the kind of body that is essential to differential color.

"No one is white before he/she came to America...It took generations, and a vast amount of coercion, before this became a white country," said James Baldwin (Baldwin 178). Talk over a few implications of this statement by Baldwin with someone else.

1. What makes the identification of a white country so important?

2. Is being an American associated with being white?

At a children's book area, I was curious to see what books might be on children and race. What caught my eyes was a book with the title "Let's Talk about Race...I'll take off my skin. Will you take off yours?". Describing races, Julius Lester sometimes frames the discussion around whose race is better. He, then, tries to get each child to imagine that they could take off their skin. "I'll take off my skin. Will you take off yours?" (Lester 2005).

Questions

1. Contrary to Lester, why take off a child's skin?

2. What are a few reasons for positively keeping a child's skin regardless of the color?

3. What would taking off one's skin do to a child identity?

As the reader, what does the message of his book by Ta-Nehisi Coates mean regarding identity, self-confidence, history, or other issues?

The spirit and soul are the body and brain, which are destructible—that is why they are so precious...In America, it is traditional to destroy the black body. It is heritage (Coates 103). The story of the black body's destruction must always begin with his or her error (Coates 96). The struggle to understand is the only advantage we have over this madness. You have been cast into a race in which the wind is always in your face and hounds are always at your heels... (Coates 107). Black life is cheap, but in America black bodies are a natural resource of incomparable value (Coates 132).

Comment

Comment on how the Black body can both be of precious value and the madness of its destruction. Dig deeply.

Subsequently, our reading turns to pinpointing our values and identity by way of an exercise, including filling in phrases and completing questions.

Reflection. Exercise

Answer the succeeding questions in a journal after pondering them as if alone in your favorite secluded location. Questions and completion exercise.

1. From a broad arena, what comes to mind when you think of social differences?

2. When you bring up feelings, what emotions surface about differences?

3. The biggest issue I have with social differences is...

4. I feel better about social difference when I...

5. I feel worse about social difference when I...

6. When I base my thoughts/feelings about social differences exclusively on my personal experiences, I recognize these dangers...

7. How have my thoughts changed about social difference through the years?

8. Considering persons within groups contributes to my...

9. Specifically, I am more comfortable with which particular groups?

    When responding, consider any of these types of groups by race, sexual orientation, ethnicity, gender, religion, social class, age or another affiliation.

10. I like my ethnic/racial group (insert name...) because...

11. I find this ethnic/racial group (insert name...) least likeable because...

12. When I consider a scale of compatibility with any groups, I rank my compatibility with them as follows:

    List five groups, then rank them with #1 being the most compatible of all groups and #5 being the least compatible of any group.

13. I think that all human groups should get along because...

14. I think that the greatest barrier to groups getting along is...

15. I think that the greatest way for groups to get along is...

16. I find little or great value in studying different groups because...

An essay and diagram on how your mind works in addressing differences

Digging deeper, we now explore the process of how your mind deals with difference. You will be doing a framing approach to how your mind works. The most challenging part of this venture may be that the central question is posed in a very general way. You may wish to re-focus the query specifically to make your response more manageable.

This basic question you will answer in a written essay will include a concluding a diagram(s) of how your mind works regarding differences.

Question: What is the thought process through which your mind goes when addressing human differences? In your dynamic thought process, you may want to consider values, beliefs, spirituality, unique experiences, group situations, biases, concepts, analysis, theories, principles, language, statistical data and/or something you have read. Of course, you will not develop a process that takes in all of the above. You may see and describe how your mind works when you consider differences. The possibilities are wide-open since you are probing your mind and its special approaches to human variability. There is no page limit on the essay.

Concluding Diagram

After you write your thought process, creatively clarify your thoughts in one or more diagrams you choose. This visualization offers a new dimension to understanding your ideas about difference.

General Identity Issues Related to Encountering Differences

Now having bundled our thoughts about difference, we can probe some related identity issues in our journals. Write a candidly as possible.

1. The greatest influences in my overall development have been...

2. I think that persons who are important in my life see me as...

3. When I am "up against a wall," I...

4. When I look in a "mirror," I see...

5. One of the blind spots about which I think I know something is...

6. I am particularly inspired by...

7. I am passionate about...

8. If I could change my identity, I would be...

9. What am I like at my core?

"Identity is a multilayered process of understanding who you are, how you are seen by others and the consequences of being seen in these ways," according to Professor Tania Mitchell. And our unique, group affiliations mold our identity in relation to gender, class, race, sexual orientation, ability, religion, language and citizenship status (Mitchell 16).

Direct Preparation for Dealing with Differences

The whole thinking process in this chapter is geared to assist your increased engagement in encountering differences. In a focused way, we shall now pursue how you can prepare for addressing social differences. Record the responses to the items below in your journal.

1. The biggest motivators for my interest in facing differences are...

2. The largest fears I have about differences are...

3. As a planner, I...

4. Among my life goals are...

5. Those who have had the most impact on my addressing differences are...

6. The top questions I need to ask about dealing with differences are...

7. What kinds of opportunities might have the best potential for significant personal and/or academic and/or professional growth?

8. How will I make my choices about dealing with differences?

9. How might my focus on status relate to issues of personal power?

Individual identity linked with structural change

In her courses, Professor Mitchell's focus on identity informs a person's relationship with social change (Mitchell 15). Referencing scholars Komives, Lucas and McMahon, she indicates that it is necessary to understand how your identity may differ from others in order to move toward...considering injustice as structural and systemic rather than an individual matter...An intentional focus on identity may...allow students to move beyond defensiveness...and guilt to recognize structural inequality...and to identify spaces where their identities can support them in actions aimed toward change (Mitchell 17).

Question

What do you think is important regarding Mitchell's views about the connection between identity and social change? Shoulder-to-shoulder, you spur on this vital pursuit of racial justice through change.

Reciprocity

To enliven the context of our perspectives of differences and race, we explore the mutual action called **reciprocity**. You may awaken to some vulnerability in this process of reciprocity. You may discover rewards and discomfort, yet it will be worth it.

In the English language, reciprocity collegially suggests an action of mutual exchange that often implies counterpart, complement or equivalent relationships (Webster's New World Dictionary and Thesaurus 531). What better way to pursue our journey than by clarifying our understanding of differences and racial transparency. This expands our curiosity and intrigue.

Consider reciprocal love. What might this mean in personal relationships?

Grappling with race can be mutually rewarding as we try to live fulfilling lives. An international expression of reciprocity follows in a Chinese context. Looking differently at reciprocity was enhanced by my studies with Mandarin Chinese.

Reciprocity is understood to mean like-hearted. Or in the question to the early Chinse philosopher Confucius, his disciple asked, "Is there one single word that one can practice throughout one's life?" The Master said, 'It is perhaps "like-hearted considerateness. What you do not wish for yourself, do not impose on others'" (Huang 156).

Think of two key issues within the Confucius information, and apply them to your current scene.

Imagine that you and I see the Chinese character meaning reciprocity. It is called **shu.** Many characters consist of two separate parts. For **shu,** the upper part **ru** means "like or same." The lower part **xin** refers to "heart, or with the same heart" (Huang 23).

Reflect about the meaning of the Chinse character **shu.**

Now focus on reciprocity in race relations. How do you picture reciprocity in your everyday racial experience? Be creative and practical.

Guide for responding to the wrap up section in each chapter

Since this following information is your new story. The flexible guidelines may offer some structure and/or stimulate the imagination.

Consider any of these suggestions:

1. Connect any ideas and/or feelings from the material in this chapter with a main issue in your life.

2. Apply any part of the chapter's material to a supervisor or other authority.

3. Relate chapter information to any outside persons who are regularly involved or coincidentally connected with you.

4. Discuss how chapter material can be affiliated with any incident or event.

5. Apply chapter material to a unique person within your experience.

6. Consider how something from this chapter relates to a family person or friend.

7. Very likely you will still have other suitable thoughts and feelings about applying chapter information. Do use them.

8. If you cannot see any applications from this chapter to your life, then fully explain why.

Wrap up, your story, and questions

In the questions below, address what feelings and thoughts are prominent as you continue to tell your story about strikes you in this chapter. For this single time, I offer a few added angles for discussing your feelings and thoughts. For a start with your discussion, consider ideas, illustrations, methods and/or techniques.

Journal what in this chapter has affected your emotions? Explain. What stimulated your thinking? Explain. Do you find any changes in your approaches to current life after progressing through the chapter? Explain. How do you think the content and/or procedures of this chapter connect with your everyday experience?

These above questions guide what becomes **you story** in each **chapter** of this book. You can always refer back to these questions found in this first chapter. Such personal information may or may not be shared.

Questions

1. Because of your experience within this chapter, what questions still emerge?

2. What else do you want to know?

Works Cited

Baldwin, James. "On Being White'...and Other Lies." ESSENCE, Edited by James Roediger. BLACK ON WHITE: BLACK WRITERS ON WHAT IT MEANS TO BE WHITE. Schocken Books, 1984, p. 178.

Bouie, Jamelle. "Racism is not a Moral Question." NYT, 14 Nov. 2021, SR7.

Chude-Solei, Louis. "Imagination." BOSTONIA, Spring-Summer 2022, p. 60.

Coates, Ta-Nehisi. BETWEEN THE WORLD AND ME. Spiegel and Grau, 2005, pp. 101, 107.

Huang, Chichung. THE ENALECTS OF CONFUCIUS, Oxford University Press, 1997, pp. 156, 23.

Lester, Julius. LET'S TALK ABOUT RACE: I'LL TAKE OFF MY SKIN. WILL YOU TAKE OFF YOURS? Harper Collins Publishers, 2005.

Mitchell, Tania. "Identity and Social Action: Self-Examination and Systemic Change." DIVERSITY AND DEMOCRACY, Fall 2015, vol. 18, no. 4, pp. 15-17.

WEBSTER'S NEW WORLD DICTIONARY AND THESAURUS, Wiley & Co., p. 531.

Chapter 2

Empathy – The Lens to Guide Dismantling Racial Experiences

Eighteen states require school programs which promote empathy and other core values. So empathy workshops and curricula are implemented in entire classrooms. When there is fighting, bullying, other types of violence, and harsh words, often teachers sit down and try to find out what is wrong instead of sending perpetrators for punishment. In several schools, the number of fights has dropped and disciplinary referrals reduced (Hu 23). Empathy even can mean problem-solving.

Introduction

We start by focusing on empathy as a lens for understanding all life. In this book, the empathic lens is powerfully designed to guide each moment and show light on all our experiences.

While we may be new to fully understanding empathy, numerous illustrations can add to your pursuit. Old habits can intervene. Attempt to not be overly critical and continue to be open to questions about what you discover. U. S. President Barack Obama and Chinese Prime Minister Wen Jia Boa are empathy advocates. Exercises and actions provide practical interactions that stimulate new understanding and growth.

Empathy

Defining empathy

Two definitions help clarify what we mean by empathy. Empathy can be defined as the capacity to share or understand the experiences of another person, including her/his thoughts, attitudes, emotions and perceptions... Everyone possesses this capacity to varying degrees, but in each person the capacity is modified or even distorted by social experiences," says Michael Rothenberg (Rothenberg 311). Or, defining empathy means to "sense what people are feeling, being able to take their perspective, and to cultivate rapport and attunement with a broad diversity of people," according to Daniel Goleman (Goleman WORKING 24).

Question

Which of the two definitions do you prefer? Explain.

Groups also have needs and moods and are situations fertile for the practice of empathy. Work team members often interact with each other in empathy. Showing each other empathy leads a "team to create and sustain positive norms and manage its relationships with the outside world more effectively" (Goleman PRIMAL 177).

Can empathy be successful in a group situation? With Goleman's team approach, a manufacturing team engaged with a maintenance department by showing empathy with it. That meant "figuring out what the whole system needs, and going after all those involved to feel satisfied in the outcomes" (Goleman PRIMAL 182-183). The manufacturing team used its skills to attempt an understanding of how the two groups affected each other, and thereby added to a jointly beneficial relationship. One action was to nominate the other group for a systemwide award. Two resonating outcomes developed. One was to build rapport between the two departments and to spotlight the success of the other group's work and esteem. Empathy across team-to-team boundaries results in organizational effectiveness (Goleman PRIMAL 182-183). And group members anticipate a leader's "supportive emotional connection – for empathy" (Goleman PRIMAL 5).

Exercise. When we are hurting, we often try to identify with each other using some of the following scramble of expressions:

My friend had that happen.	I'm trying to feel your pain.	I am here for you.
I sense your feeling.	That's tough.	
Thanks for sharing.	You will get over it.	Oh, no.
I hear you. That's huge.	Bummer.	I know just how you feel.

Next, select two phrases about empathy from the scramble above and journal/discuss your thoughts and feelings about using those words/ expressions. You might choose an expression that is generically preferred and select one that you find least appropriate. You may want to consider other expressions.

Empathy Versus Sympathy

Sympathy, on the other hand, also shows concern about another person's condition (Stotland 247). Yet, sympathy should not be mixed up with empathy. Sympathy is the ability to apprehend suffering or pain, to perceive or understand it. "In sympathy I know you are in pain, and I sympathize with you, but I feel my sympathy and my pain, not your anguish and your pain." I feel my pain, not yours when I say, "I'm sorry" (Sills 441).

Sympathy often conjures up someone's death. The sharing of a few genuine words is what connects, rather than spontaneous clichés and platitudes. The three-point model of Millicent Fenwick can serve as a guide. 1. Expressing sympathy as in "I'm sorry..." 2. Sharing something about the deceased. 3. Comforting words such as "Loving friends..." Editor Jane Lear's favorite sympathetic response occurred at the time of her brother's death. "My Dear Jane..."IT STINKS" (Feiler ST2).

Acknowledging that sympathy cards can be sent weeks after the death, Fenwick also clarifies that there is general agreement that a condolence note is "an obligation of friendship." Emily Post affirms that sending an email or commenting on a public forum is only an acceptable first gesture. Strikingly, 90 percent of sympathy cards are purchased by people over 40 (Feiler ST2).

Questions

1. What new ways could you express sympathy?

2. Do the "I'm sorry" expressions often try to substitute for empathy. Explain.

Empathy Across Similarities

It is essential to "present other's experiences and beliefs from their point of view. Empathy, in more recent times, has popularly meant identifying with similar experiences of others (Ridley 28). We often hear of putting ourselves in the shoes of someone else. Some college students have been adamant that empathy only means similarity with others (Grose 2007).

Explore how persons have tried to show empathy across similarities. Think about these mostly real-life experiences.

My friend's teenage son had been confined to bed with cancer for several months. A family acquaintance visited them in their home. He said to the parents, "I know how you feel. My brother struggled with cancer, too."

In a popular TV comedy series, the apartment manager sees that a new resident is experiencing considerable difficulty in the big move. The manager says, "Mary, I know just how you feel." She responds, "No, you don't, Phyllis. I don't even know how I feel."

Questions with Journaling

1. What questions do you have about these illustrations?

2. What feelings and thoughts could be present for the persons receiving attempts at empathy?

3. In what ways are the persons who are trying to connect mainly drawing attention to themselves?

4. Does empathy only take place when you express your experiential similarities with the similarities of someone else? Explain.

5. What is a central difference between empathy and sympathy?

Empathy Across Differences

It is also essential to understand empathy across differences. These examples show major challenges for the use of empathy across differences.

In July, 2016, a white Brooklyn police officer reflects on his law enforcement work. "You can't have a perspective on this job, unless you do it...Unless you're in policing, doing it every day as a career, you can't know what it's like" (Rojas 19).

And just before ending an intense, classroom-discussion among African American, Asian American and white students, a sudden change occurred. The conversation between a white, male authoritarian-type student and a black, confident-male student heated to a boil. In apparent frustration, the African American said, "You'll never understand what it is like to be African American!!!" He gathered his belongings and left the room (Grose 1998).

1. Think about how empathy could have been used in these two situations. What deep issues/feelings can you address?

2. Think of some empathic words that you could carefully use in each of the two situations.

3. Which one of these two types of experiences could be particularly challenging to engage others with empathy? Explain.

Empathy can be illustrated by a physician-patient relationship. Until her transformative journey with empathy, Dr. Pauline Chen only thought of herself as "just a surgeon and not – or so I thought – someone who needed to linger in the shoes of the dying." As a colleague stated, "This is a part of the problem of being trained to be disease-oriented rather than patient-oriented" (Chen 95, 133, 175).

Dr. Chen's overall change happened when she was inspired by the empathic care of the dying and their families by a respected colleague. She no longer slipped away from her ICU patients and families.

> I would bring them to their loved one's bedside and close the curtains around not them but us…I would touch family members, embrace those who looked particularly lost, and tell them of the final comfort of their presence. The honor of worrying – of caring, of easing suffering, of being present – may be our most important task (Chen 101, 211, 217).

Dr. Chen wished she could have done more. Then she realized she had done more. Beyond the comforting and easing of suffering, she said that she "had been present for them during life and despite of death." The process of dying could be cast in terms of opportunities. The interpersonal, emotional expressions are the "final gifts of the medical revolution of the last century" (Chen 160, 211).

Each of us can empathize with everyone at any time not only in circumstances like those of Dr. Chen (WISPE 441). The following observation is by two educators. "It is dangerous to start by thinking how the other person's experience is similar to my own. The other person is the central figure/actor." The other educator said, "Their feelings are the source of my empathy and the object of my empathy" (Nord and Haynes 50).

Questions

1. What were keys to Dr. Chen's transformation?

2. In what you have heard, or experienced, do you think that doctors generally follow Dr. Chen's new empathic approach? Explain.

Can empathy be approached across the differences with negative persons? This kind of range of persons includes those who are timid bigots to a perceived enemy.

A bigot displays intolerant beliefs and attitudes which may provoke discriminatory actions (WEBSTER'S NEW WORLD 60). A part of sociologist Robert Merton's typology focuses on unequal treatment of racial groups. A timid bigot may not discriminate if discrimination costs money, reduces profits or is pressured by peers or the government to not act. But the "all-weather bigot unhesitatingly acts on prejudicial beliefs…" (Schaefer 37). And the most subtle bigot is called a respectable bigot. This person may tell questionable jokes about Polish or Scandinavian Americans but hold back from joking about people of color (Schaefer 126).

Role Playing

The reader can create a scenario about empathic communications with a bigot, a white supremacist or an enemy. The setting would be with an individual or with members of a small group. While it might be more comfortable to begin empathic role-playing about bigots than extremists, the empathic principles would be similar. The empathic exchanges could be from tolerant persons toward the extremists. Safety issues would be paramount when communicating with potentially violent extremists.

Nonverbally, the unarmed empathic person could attempt friendly smiles, with arms at one's sides, and maybe wearing a peaceful-type T-shirt. No flags. With assertiveness, a tolerant persons could initiate expressions like "I am_____ and how do you want to be called?" "I am curious about sensitive human differences. What do you think about social differences?" "I hear you." "Do you want to be treated by others as you would treat them?" (Golden Rule) "What is your story about racial experiences?" "I am trying to put myself in your place as you have experienced racial differences." "You know that our different skin colors are just what we are all given. It's how we feel about difference that counts." How might you show empathy at the end of the conversation?

Remember that empathy is not judgmental nor persuasive. It is to encourage an understanding relationship.

The Process of Empathic Choices – Informed Empathy – Empathic Action – Possible Change

Importance of Empathic Choices

A psychological belief is that empathy is a choice. Persons can be intentionally motivated to select empathy for groups of persons different from their own, for example, gays and lesbians. Our expansion of empathy, and the limits of it, are what we choose (Cameron et al. SR12).

The practice of empathy is of crucial importance. "We have all felt the empathy of a sensitive teacher or friend; we have all been struck by its absence in an unfeeling coach or boss" (Goleman 49).

Even a Chinese Prime Minister, Wen Jia Bao, showed empathy for earthquake victims as he toured devastated Chinese sites. He "shared tearful moments with newly orphaned children." In popular lore he is called "Grandpa Wen" (Jacobs A6).

And maybe, the listing of our skills in empathy can be valuable on our resumes. The CEO of a communication technology company discussed in 2015 the qualities he wants in workers. "Empathy is a big one...If you have no ability to empathize, then it is difficult to give people feedback, and it's difficult to help people improve. Everything becomes harder" (Bryant BU2).

Also, recent scholarly studies have shown attention to empathy on social media. Psychologist, Dr. Larry Rosen's research team, found that "virtual empathy was positively correlated with real-world empathy." Sadly, this article's writer also remarks that some parts of the social media are still often a pit of hatred, intolerance and bullying" (Wayne ST2).

Of course, empathy is vital for counseling therapy and psychodrama. Empathy has consistently been identified as "one of the most important and necessary conditions of effective therapy" (Yanive73; Pedersen and Hernandez 6).

1. It has been said, "Empathy without reason is blind." How does that idea relate to our choices? (Trout 6).

2. Do we still need to pursue our emotions that are needed for empathy? Deeply explain.

3. Why do you think that there is great variety in the ability of persons to use empathy?

Informed Empathy

This is a disability definition of informed empathy. "Informed empathy means acknowledging the limitations associated with persons with disabilities and appreciating the impact these issues can have on individuals, families and those providing care" (Miller 114, 125). And, consider this generic definition. Informed empathy is an intentional approach which takes on the experience of others from their perspectives and feelings, and may stimulate individual and group responses (Grose 2017).

Ninian Smart wants us to present other's experiences from their point of view...suspending our own values...and being morally neutral. We can turn to their stories, art, traditions and institutions. It is essential to present others' experience and beliefs from their point of view...suspending our own values. In trying to hear and see from inside persons' hearts and minds, we can turn to their stories, art, traditions and institutions. We attempt to think and feel with others while being morally neutral (Smart XXIII).

Questions

1. Considering Smart's perspective, how challenging is it to "suspend our values" and be "morally neutral?"

2. How do you think or feel about Smart's approach? Can you use it his way? Explain.

The current breadth of practicing informed empathy throughout the world can be observed in teacher education training, medical programs, religious organizations, local governments, theaters, and schools among others. Two hundred and forty-seven cities have committed to practicing informed empathy. They have accepted this call from The Charter for Compassion, which says: "We call upon all men and women... to cultivate an informed empathy with the suffering of all human beings, even those regarded as enemies" (CHARTER 3).

One Protestant denomination, the Presbyterian Church, U.S.A., affirmed their commitment to informed empathy in 2010. They want their youth to have accurate information about other traditions, religions and cultures (Parsons 2010). The Presbyterian's commitment to informed empathy is intertwined with compassion (Turkovich 1).

Added clarification can result from two goals that are essential for democratic education, or education for democracy – informed empathy and "skepticism"... according to honored educator Deborah Meier. She highlighted the term informed empathy in the 1990s. It was in the Meier's schools for democracy that students learned the art of living together as citizens. As a joint venture of teachers and parents as allies, Meier advocated knowing the background of students. And through full openness and unlimited questions, children and adults experienced mutual learning (Meier 272).

The Scarsdale, New York, Middle School's commitment to informed empathy not only encourages problem-solving but also develops group rapport. Consultant David Levine has been teaching/practicing empathy within this school. Some students say that mean girls will be mean, and boys will still knock books out of one another's hands outside classrooms. Yet, some are trying not to put down classmates nor call them "moron" or "idiot." And that middle-school student council is committed to change student culture. Many parents praise the new focus, while some think that parents should also be trained. It is beginning "to stick" at Scarsdale (Hu 1, 23).

Other writers state that "building a culture of informed empathy means asking young people to imagine what kind of world they want to create...and work to understand each other without social dominance structuring these relationships" (Verner 77). And so, informed empathy is designed so students "can see a fuller range of conditions and begin questioning social inequity" (Ladson-Billings 234).

Teacher-education scholar Nadine Dolby challenged her students to look beyond sending toys to Haitian children. They needed money for medical supplies and food to address survival within acute poverty. Dolby told her students that the real work of informed empathy is to "stretch oneself into the reality of one whose experience was very far from my own." Informed empathy is the gateway to hope and joy. That means asking difficult questions (Dolby 76).

Questions

1. How important are the background conditions of a person when empathy experiences arise?

2. How viable is the timing issue when informed empathy takes place?

3. In what ways can students stretch themselves empathically into unfamiliar reality?

4. What is the empathic value for students to explore questioning social inequality? Note above illustration.

5. What is the role of empathy in problem-solving?

6. Are you persuaded that informed empathy can encourage citizenship in democracy? See above.

7. Does informed empathy simply confuse a complicated experience? Explain.

8. How is it possible to genuinely practice informed empathy toward enemies? Explain.

Empathic Action

Therefore, empathy can be combined with social action and social change. This suggests that informed empathy involves more than basic, personal transformation. For example, "What needs to be done about global change?" That question puts us at a high level of empathic complexity (Dolby 76-78).

Consider, too, that empathy can be called revolutionary or radical. This is the viewpoint of Professor Anita Novak, who states that our innate capacity of empathy can leverage for social change (Novak 179). When considering the needs of people and the planet, this empathic action is a "practical way to change the way society is run" (Novak 73). We can move from reflection to action for "the purpose of positive, sustainable social justice" (Novak 151).

As a consequence of Novak's research at McGill University, she used empathy in action to improve business practices in Toronto, Canada. When Novak takes informed empathy to the dynamic dimension of action, it is identified as empathic action.

The next empathy in action illustration magnifies what an individual can do to affect structural, social change. That includes legislation. Empathy in action for attorney Amy Klobuchar's infant daughter and thousands of other infants, and their mothers, was a turning point for medical care for all races. At birth, Klobuchar's daughter was unable to swallow. And, medical procedures dramatically manipulated the infant's swallowing. But by the end of the 24-hour hospital stay, the nurse told Klobuchar that policies dictated that she "get out." Quickly moving to a nearby motel, Klobuchar then had to nurse her child every three hours, back and forth between the two locations (Fisher 9).

Upset over the experience, Klobuchar advocated at the Minnesota legislature for a law to force health plans to allow new mothers to stay in a hospital for 48 hours rather than only a 24-hour period. If there are complications as in Klobuchar daughter's inability to swallow at birth, the mother is insured another day that makes a huge difference. Insurance companies tried to delay the passage of the law (Fisher 9).

For her timely legislative hearing, she recruited six of her pregnant friends to join her during the eight-minute hearing. "Klobuchar was charming, engaged and funny," declared David Schultz, a Hamline University professor (Fisher 9). A few months later, the 1995 Minnesota law passed. The federal law only applies to coverage provided with employer insurance. President Clinton signed that law in 1996 (Fisher 10).

In another illustration, we can experience empathy up close and even in the pit of our stomachs. Leaders, like Mayor Jeff Jacobs of St. Louis Park, Minnesota, have literally become "conversant with sensitive issues surrounding the physical, emotional and social difficulties of poverty and food insecurity caused by living on food stamps for even one week…Could you eat for 43 cents per day for one week?" Mayor Jacobs took that challenge and found that raisins became a "luxury" he had to forgo on his new budget. Steve Hunegs, Executive Director of Jewish Community Relations Council of Minnesota and Dakotas, said, "The food stamp diet gives you empathy in a small way for those surviving on practically nothing…I can opt out at any time" (Stapelton 1).

Questions

Journal for greater insight and meaning

1. Engaging injustice is empathy in action. Why do you think that the idea of empathy with social action has not gained more widespread consideration?

2. What are a few other challenges in which you could pursue empathic action?

3. What were several factors that contributed to Klobuchar's empathy in action?

4. How could you use those factors to promote getting your issues through a level of government?

Problem-solving

A hard-core veteran sat down in my office to complain about his B+ that he earned on an assignment in a graduate race relations class. Normally he earned A's. He sat between me and the door. After 10-15 minutes of discussion with the door he closed, he brought out a large pocket knife and opened the blade. He fiddled with it as our interaction continued for another 10-15 minutes. My empathy continued within increased tension. I tried to connect with his student disappointment while also thinking about how to get him to leave. I do not remember what convinced him to leave. Maybe he was convinced that I was the one who determines grades and I was not budging. We were both increasingly weary. After he finally left, I went to campus physician for a basic checkup!

Questions

1. What empathic actions do you think I could have taken to further alleviate the tension?

2. Think of a few specific words I could have used in that approach with empathy.

3. My questions – Where was the secretary? Would an outside phone call have helped me?

Limits of empathy

I am stuck in my fear of not doing empathy right.

I can frustrate and hurt the vulnerable by assuming too much and exaggerating my understanding.

I underestimate the value and effect of empathy.

I sympathize, saying "I'm sorry," when I know that it is about my feelings.

I am physically present with hurting person(s) without understanding or thinking about what my presence can mean to the other(s).

I can have the opportunity to empathize but not take it.

I am insincere, saying for example, "I know exactly how you feel."

I use a cliché like "I feel your pain."

I am hurtful when saying, "You have got to let it go. Move on."

I do not believe in the empathy of others because I do not believe it works for me.

I negate the use of empathizing across differences because I only understand empathy as identifying across similarities.

I just do not choose to show empathy.

I think that expressing empathy is too complex.

Benefits of empathy

I can enhance and build relationships.

I can promote mutuality and gratitude.

I can expose any kind of privilege.

I can address egoism, sexism, racism, ableism, ageism, heterosexism, ethnocentrism and other isms.

I can reduce tension and conflict.

I can attend to hurt and suffering.

I can awaken and release hope and joy.

I can elevate self-esteem.

I can enlighten and empower decision making.

I can activate and strengthen courageous followership.

I can support and help authenticate resonate leadership.

I can promote team rapport, cooperation and identity.

I can cultivate cross-cultural understanding and appreciation.

I can increase the effectiveness of helping professionals.

I can help release us from avoidance, suppression and guilt.

I can enlighten politicians.

I can promote justice and peace throughout daily living.

I can reduce the gap of indifference to social change.

When intentionally informed, I can open hidden contexts and perspectives.

Exercise. Practicing the Possible

Consider when empathy could be shared with persons experiencing joy, frustration or sorrow. Consider only choosing one, like frustration? Journal a few of the words you might say to the other person. Plus, clarify for yourself how you might be present in empathy with someone. Next, look for actual situations where empathy can be shown. Then, actually, practice it. Afterwards, ask yourself a few questions. How effective were the attempts to empathize? What cues did the other person offer about the attempts with empathy? What lessons did you learn about your approaches to empathy?

Conclusion

Empathy exhibits two key features: trying to express vicarious feeling for the other, and attempting to take the perspective of another. Empathy, in essence, focuses on the other person and/or group and not oneself. Profound, potent and practical are empathy's effects particularly when expressed with utmost care and potential spontaneity. Many persons and groups practice empathy, and informed empathy, without identifying it. It is important to clarify that empathy is being expressed, so we can build on it.

Wrap up, my story and questions

Journal what feelings and thoughts are prominent as you continue to tell your story with empathy. For this single time, I offer a few added angles for discussing your feelings and thoughts about the chapter. What stimulated your thinking? Explain. For a start, consider ideas, illustrations, methods and/or techniques. Next, what in this chapter has affected your emotions? Explain. Plus, do you find changes in your approaches to empathy after engaging information in this chapter? Explain. In this final link to your story with empathy, how do you think the content and methods this chapter apply to every-day life?

For this one time, I suggest how this chapter might prepare yourself for real experiences with people of color? Imagine that empathy is relevant for experiences with roommates, family, co-workers, classmates, neighbors. If you might have more empathy toward persons with whom you feel comfortable, would that mean you need to begin practicing empathy with them? Or, would you grow more if you choose to express empathy where you now feel little connection with persons? Identify the person(s) with whom you might show empathy. (This information need not be shared.) Ponder why that person is a suitable starting point for you. Later, you may empathize in a real-life situation.

Questions

1. How do perceive that you could enhance your approaches to empathy. Journal.

2. When in doubt, is it enough to just be present with the other person? Explain.

3. Under what circumstances can empathy be used for problem-solving? Respond specifically though not necessarily comprehensively.

4. Evaluate your ability for empathy.

5. How do cultural similarities and differences influence the empathy process? (That might include relating to Latinos, Asian Americans, Indigenous persons, Black Americans, whites.)

Works Cited

Bryant, Adam. "Is Empathy on Your Resume?" NYT, 12 July. 2015, p. BU2.

Cameron, Daryl, et al. "Empathy Is Actually a Choice," NYT, 12 July. 2015, p. SR12.

Charterforcompassion.org

Chen, Pauline. FINAL EXAM. Alfred Knopf, pp. 101, 160, 211, 217.

Dolby, Nadine. RETHINKING MULTICULTURAL EDUCATION FOR THE NEXT GENERATION: THE NEW EMPATHY AND SOCIAL JUSTICE. Routledge Publishers, 2012.

Feiler, Bruce. "The Art of Condolence," NYT, 2 Oct. 2016, p. ST2.

Fisher, Marc. "Amy Klobuchar was Kicked Out of the Hospital 24 Hours after Giving Birth. Her Outrage Fueled Her Political Rise." WASHINGTON POST, 21 Jan. 2020, p. 9.

Golden Rule

Goleman, Daniel, et al. PRIMAL LEADERSHIP. Harvard Business Review Press, 2002, pp. 182-185.

—, WORKING WITH EMOTIONAL INTELLIGENCE. Bantam Books, 1998, p. 5.

Grose, Charles. Sociology class, Fall Term, 2007, Normandale Community College, Bloomington, Minnesota.

—, Educational Foundations class, Oct., Mankato State University, Minnesota.

Hu, Winnie. "Schools' Gossip Girls and Boys Get Some Lessons in Empathy." NYT, 5 Apr. 2009, p. 23.

Jacobs, Andrew. "In Quake, Apotheosis of Premier 'Grandpa.'" NYT, 21 May. 2008, p. A6.

Johnson, Ron. Speech at Greater Grace Church, Melisa Harris TV Program, MSNBC, 17 Aug. 2015, Ferguson, Missouri.

Ladson-Billings, Gloria. "Preparing Teachers for Diverse Student Populations." REVIEW OF RESEARCH IN EDUCATION, Vol 224, 1999, p. 234.

Lucas, Ashley. "The Will to Ride," Guthrie Theater Program, Minneapolis, Vol 54, Issue 2, p. 13.

Meier, Deborah. "Supposing That," PHI DELTA KAPPAN. Dec. 1996, Vol 78, Issue 4, p. 272.

Miller, Sonya. "A Curriculum Focused on Informed Empathy Improves Attitudes Toward Persons with Disabilities," PERSPECT MEDICAL EDUCATION, 2 June. 2013, pp. 114, 125.

Nord, William and Charles Haynes. "Taking Religion Seriously Across the Curriculum," First Amendment Center, Nashville, 1998, p. 50.

Novak, Anita. "Introducing a Pedagogy of Empathic Action as Informed by Social Entrepreneurs." doctoral dissertation, McGill University, 30 June. 2011.

Parsons, Gradye. Letter of the General Assembly, Presbyterian Church, U.S. A., 10 Aug. 2010.

Pedersen, Paul and Daniel Hernandez. A GUIDEBOOK FOR LEARNING COUNSELING ACROSS CULTURES. Thousand Oaks, Fourth Edition, 1996.

Pedersen, Paul, et al. (editors). COUNSELING ACROSS CULTURES. Sage Publications, 1996, pp. 28, 39.

Ridley, Charles and Danielle Lingle. "Cultural Empathy in Multicultural Counseling," in Rojas, Rick. "One Shift: Officers Patrol an Anxious America," NYT, 24 July. 2016, p. 19.

Rothenberg, Michael. ENCYCLOPEDIA AMERICANA. 2006, p. 311.

Schanzenbach Canham, Julie (editor) MINNESOTA FOOD SHARE, Vol 11, No 5, Autumn 2007, p.1.

Sills, David. (editor). "Sympathy and Empathy," THE INTERNATIONAL ENCYCLOPEDIA OF THE SOCIAL SCIENCES. Crowell Collier Macmillan, Vol 15, 1968.

Smart, Roderick Ninian. DIMENSIONS OF THE SACRED. University of California Press, 1996, xxiii.

Solomon, Deborah. "Dr. Feel It." NEW YORK TIMES MAGAZINE, 01 Feb. 2009, p. 11.

Stapelton, Kristin King. "Surviving on Practically Nothing: The Food Stamp Diet Challenge."

Stotland, Ezra. "Empathy and Sympathy," in Kuper, Adam and Jessica Kuper. SOCIAL SCIENCE ENCYCLOPEDIA. Routledge, 01 Jan. 2004.

Trout, J. D. WHY EMPATHY MATTERS. Penguin Group, 2009, p. 7.

Turkovich, Marilyn. "Charter of Compassion International Newsletter," 12 Jan. 2016, p. 1.

Verner, Sharon, et al. THE ARTS AND DISTINCTIVE BE-LINGUAL YOUTH. Routledge Publishers, 2013.

Wayne, Teddy. "Found on Facebook: Empathy." NYT, 11 Oct. 2015, p. ST2.

WEBSTER'S NEW WORLD DICTIONARY. Wiley Publishers, 2002, p. 60.

Wispe, L. G. "Empathy." INTERNATIONAL ENCYCLOPEDIA of SOCIAL SCIENCE, Vol 15, 1968.

Yaniv, Dani. "Dynamic of Creativity and Empathy in Role Reversal: Contributions from Neuroscience." REVIEW OF GENERAL PSYCHOLOGY, Mar. 2012, p. 73.

Chapter 3

Advantage and Privilege Focused through the Lens of Peggy McIntosh's "Invisible Knapsack"

Privilege and socio-economic class - "The Titanic"

Consider the life/death costs of economic privilege shown in the film "The Titanic." How curious are we about the consequences of economic privilege for those on that "unsinkable" ocean liner? The lifeboats could only accommodate 1,178 of the 2,207 passengers and crew on board. (Newman 291) The tenor of the NEW YORK TIMES front-page headline changed just four days after the Titanic hit the iceberg. The headline read: "Many Needlessly Died on Titanic." Information surfaced about the number of unfilled lifeboats (NYT 2).

The life boats were accessible from the first and second-class class decks near the wealthier passengers. Locked doors and other barriers prevented the steerage passengers from freely moving to the upper decks during the entire voyage. Those in steerage were given little help during the disaster and even some were forcibly kept from escaping by sailors standing guard. In today's society, the economically privileged have "easy access to various 'life boats' in times of social or economic disaster; others face locked gates, segregated decks and policies that make even survival exceedingly difficult" (Newman 291).

Introduction

In this chapter, we shall penetrate the precarious and perilous precipices of privilege, see it for what it is, and how it can be dismantled and de-energized. Many of my items offer background information.

Definitions of Privilege

Privilege is an unearned advantage gained "by birth, social position or special concession..." (RANDOM 1541). And it may be an "immunity, benefit or exemption (HERITAGE 1396). We may hear phrases like a privileged childhood, favored class, privileged position or a "silver spoon" background. Frequently unnoticed is the fact that people create organizations, institutions, policies, structures, hierarchies, and experiences that make privilege both possible and transformable (Lenski 45,74-75; Johnson 25-36).

Author's Birth Privileges/Advantages

I affirm that my birth privileges are ongoing to this moment. Selected are several general components that overlap specific privileged items. Middle class is a general item that is followed by a few economic citations. Further, feeling secure shopping in stores could be clarified by not being followed while shopping.

My long list indicates how profound is my life-time of overall privilege. A brief spontaneous response to my privilege can be generalized as white, male, heterosexual. As **I marked all the items below**, begin identifying your potential areas of privilege.

Mark items (30 options)

☐ White	☐ Diverse jobs/career opportunities
☐ Male	☐ Housing comfort
☐ European heritage	☐ U.S. secure
☐ Citizen birth	☐ Protected neighborhood
☐ Political appropriate	☐ Available healthcare
☐ Role-modeled parents	☐ Christian heritage
☐ College-educated parents	☐ English as a main language
☐ H.E. admission secure	☐ Climate stable area
☐ Educational resources at home	☐ Free Parks
☐ Middle class	☐ Roads maintained
☐ Financial security	☐ Entertainment availability
☐ Secure shopper	☐ Multiple community services
☐ Heterosexual	☐ Cultural options
☐ Duo parents	☐ Transportation independence
	☐ Other

Questions

1. Journal which of the author's checked items seem most harmful or brutal when indirectly or directly connected to privilege?

2. As the reader, what do you infer about the above kinds of privilege-related items that may have relevance for you, and others?

Questions

Use empathy, insight and perception

Attempting to look into my mind, let us deal with the succeeding questions related to my privilege? No journaling is needed.

1. Were the limited number of home invitations by Black faculty due to not wanting to address the complications of my privilege?

2. By associating with and reaching out to the Black community, did that contribute to my acceptance as a member of a Black church and a Black club? Explain in terms of privilege.

3. What might be some of the attitudes articulated by persons in the white community about my use of privilege (dominance, central norms and identity) in the Black community?

4. What were issues for me as a white member of a Black college in terms of housing options? Why did a realtor change his mind about not making the availability to purchase a house for my family in a white area of Austin, Texas?

5. Why was the college dean nominating me as the head of the sociology department other than white privilege when I first arrived?

6. What are reasons today for the continuance of historically-Black colleges?

Peggy McIntosh and the "Invisible Knapsack"

Peggy McIntosh framed the brilliant idea of white privilege as an "Invisible Knapsack" in 1988. Her wake-up-call came when, as an adult, she realized that she had been broadly taught not to see that she had white privilege, and that put her at an important advantage over people of color. She emphasized that her list of 46 unearned advantages is only about her own experience by contrast with the experiences of her African-American colleagues in the same building and in the same line of work (McIntosh 2018).

As a part of the white dominant group, she did not perceive herself as a racist, because she thought of racism as individual meanness rather than systemic injustices (McIntosh, "White" 3).

She came to "believe that white privilege, rather than discrimination, is the central actor...that creates racism and keeps it in place" (McIntosh, "Spend" 2). People of color are oppressed and fully grasp that an understanding of white privilege validates their views that there are different sets of rules for them than for white people (Sehgal 12).

Individual white persons did not invent the oppressive system and are not to be blamed and shamed for its existence. It is society that covers all whites with unsolicited, unearned advantages from birth (McIntosh, "White" 3). Refer to the systems of education, business, the law, healthcare, and money.

There are many kinds of privilege – owing to gender, race, age, religion, class, ability, sexual orientation and more. Some businesses, academic institutions, religious groups and other non-profits have been embracing the approach to privilege that McIntosh instigated 30 years ago (Schaefer 116-118).

McIntosh's identification of white privilege as an "Invisible Knapsack" has caught on broadly and is complemented by a profound reflection/action program that is connected to a project for teachers that she founded in 1987. It is called Seeking Educational Equity and Diversity (SEED). It addresses equity and inclusion through a process of teacher-led seminars. It confronts systems of oppression while deepening college and school curricula, and teaching methods, to foster more inclusive communities. SEED participants came to understand that they can be transformed when they share "their own stories of oppression and privilege..." Fears are reduced while compassion and empathy are increased (McIntosh, "Myths" 6-7). Currently, SEED has projects in 42 states, 15 other countries with at least 2,200 teachers who lead year-long seminars (Wellesley 2018).

Questions

1. What is key to the success of the SEED program?

2. How challenging may it be for teachers to participate in SEED?

The dynamics of McIntosh's own experiences with privilege and her commentary

After reading about McIntosh's wake-up call, consider her own list of experiences with privilege. Be open to more clarity about your own experiences with privilege.

Now trek through this next section with fresh eyes. It includes a few selections from McIntosh's 26-item list, and a commentary. You may wish to take notes about her information. Toward the end of this section, you will be asked to reflect upon the information and journal thoughts about your experience within the privilege system.

Exercise

Ponder these selected items from McIntosh's list. See how she identified some conditions of white privilege in her daily experience. Think about whether any of those experiences are relevant to you.

4. I can go shopping alone most the time, pretty well assured that I will not be followed or harassed.

8. If a traffic cop pulls me over or if the IRS audits my tax return, I can be sure I haven't been singled out because of my race.

1. If I should need to move, I can be pretty sure of renting or purchasing housing in an area which I can afford and in which I would want to live.

24. If my day, week or year is going badly, I need not ask of each negative episode or situation whether it has racial overtones.

12. I can swear, or dress in second-hand clothes, or not answer letters, without having people attribute these choices to the bad morals, the poverty, or the illiteracy of my race.

26. I can choose a blemish cover or bandages in so-called "flesh" color and have them more or less match my skin.

Exercise

Now, ponder two of McIntosh's statements on education from items number 6 and 7 on her list.

6. "When I am told about national heritage or about "civilization," I am shown that people of my color made it what it is."

7. "I can be sure that my children will be given curricular materials that testify to the existence of their race." (All racial and ethnic groups.)

Exercise on the Reader's List of Privileges

Now, begin journaling about your own list of specific privileges. Be spontaneous and in the moment. You may use your candor broadly. At some points, probing deeply can unearth rewarding moments and experiences. Your flexibility also may call for a break from which you may return with new enlightenment and exposure. Avoidance, denial, guilt, deception and distraction can be eliminated. All this means you pull up courage with surprising power and revealing understanding. Let's get after it!

Social Systems

Our social systems are created by persons and people who are clustered into key institutions – schools, families, economic arrangements, political schemes, government structures, entertainment industries, religious associations, among others. Our social systems likewise coordinate and organize other elements within each system. They may have their own hierarchies, policies, staff, personnel expectations, crystalized power mechanisms, any number of subgroups, and of course a variety of persons who make up their particular profiles and histories.

Theorist Alan Johnson and Peggy McIntosh understand white privilege as a social system in which individuals participate (Johnson 96-112; McIntosh, Personal Interview). McIntosh became aware of the social systems that worked to her advantage. Through the systems of privilege and power, she learned to "know better where we came from, who and where we are, and what we can do" (McIntosh, "Spend" 8).

Defining the Social System

The collection of our society's components and the relationship among them create a human social system. Many parts makeup a connected whole. Author Jodi Pfarr, recommends the major parts that are evident in all social systems. We are involved in local organizations like businesses, schools, hospitals, police departments, and stores. And we live in communities of different sizes like neighborhoods, towns, cities, states or provinces, and countries. And finally, laws and policies govern our individual, community and organizational parts. Inclusively, those interactive components form our social system (Pfarr and Allison 8).

So there are educational, economic, political, religious, athletic, artistic, medical, and other social systems. Many of them personally interact with you and me each day, although often specifically unseen and with latent power. Resolutely, those powerful systems control and describe our daily and long-term privilege.

Questions

1. What stands out for you as you dig deeply into the complexity of social systems?

2. Explain the power of systems?

3. How can you not be overwhelmed and feel distant from our systems? Journal.

Prominent Individuals

The operation of an individual can profoundly influence the social system. An individual often responds to a system and is able to make decisions within it at the local level.

An individual can affect the system when organized for power at the highest levels of systems and they are in the highest strategic areas, which carry inordinate status, respect and support. This includes political leaders such as presidents, prime ministers and international figures Nelson Mandella and Eleanor Roosevelt. Economic leaders like the director of the U.S. federal reserve and Karl Marx are noted. Religious leaders could be represented by a Pope, Martin Luther, Gandhi, Buddha, Muhammad, and Jesus. In education, leaders like Margaret Mead and Malala Yousafzai stand out. Medically transformative leaders include inventors Marie Curie and Jonas Saulk. Other inventors are represented by Thomas Edison, Johannes Gutenberg, and the Wright brothers - Orville and Wilbur. And the list goes on with nutrition inventor George Washington Carver, and the inventor of the wheel.

Finally, individuals connected to groups are necessary to challenge and change social systems. Major forces like social movements, economic depressions, political revolutions, and inordinate military upheavals greatly impact social systems.

Each individual can actively decide with groups to change the world

Therefore, transformative leaders do change social systems that contribute to everyday privilege.

Questions

1. What are the strengths of those system-changing leaders?

2. What are the common components that those kinds of leaders who hold extraordinary areas of power?

3. Briefly ruminate on how the influence of those system-changing leaders can be long-lasting?

Three Characteristics of Privilege

All our lives work within privilege, oppressions and power forces that function only through our social systems. And we, individuals and groups, effect and respond to our social systems, knowingly and without thought (Johnson 96).

Race occurs in systems which have three characteristics. They are "dominated by privileged groups, identified with privileged groups, and centered on privileged groups (Johnson 96). In our U.S. setting, those dominating-privileged leaders are white men.

Dominance

When leadership positions of power are occupied by persons within that group, Johnson maintains that the "system is dominated by a privileged group." This does not mean that most white men are powerful. And none of those men in power positions have powerful personalities (Johnson 97-99). In our U.S. setting, those dominating-privileged leaders are white men.

Identified with Privilege

Those privileged men are identified as white. Since people of color are not identified as privileged, they identify as subordinates (Johnson 102-104). For example, Blacks form their own clubs and may be linked with Black colleges. I served for 10 years in various faculty capacities in a Black college as a white-privileged male. And I was seen as a person of power in the outside dominant-white community and within that power structure. Yet the power within the college was very localized although I worked within the Black power structure of the college. Within the larger community, a Black college was largely considered invisible (Johnson 102-104).

Privilege at the Center

Many of the dominating norms in our privileged-centered culture are from our white culture. Our political system has adapted from the British-colonial commonwealth. Our Constitution is a case in point. Our white Christian faiths and churches set the standard for our whole religious life. According to Johnson, the frontpage of our newspapers predominate with pictures, discussions and quotes related to the culture of white men. To be newsworthy and get attention from the white media, marginalized groups and persons must be accepted by the power and authority of the white media (Johnson 107-110).

Exercise

Select an institution with which you are familiar, small or large. See how many of the elements or components listed in the three areas above, you can illustrate. Concentrate on basics. Remember that these institutions are not going away and they are essential to the ebb and flow of the broader systems.

Costs of Privilege

Consider our economic resources. Can we change the size of the economic "pie?" Have you ever thought of a bigger "pie?" A rigid "pie" only adds to the cost of privilege. An "'open secret of white racism is a system of institutional human waste that this society cannot afford'" (Feagin and Vera 21). See the entire book by Feagin and Vera on the waste of privilege and racism (Feagin and Vera, WHITE RACISM).

What are the **economic** costs of privilege?

We move forward to selectively choose the costs of privilege through the lens of economic power. For example, poverty is often hidden in someone else's neighborhood, and it may be publicly visible as homelessness. "The causes of homelessness in the United State are typically institutional ones: stagnating wages, changes in welfare programs, and perhaps most important, lack of affordable housing...The poorest 20% of income earners spend about 78% of their wages on housing" (Newman 308).

In order to address the costs for the poor, we present Heather McGhee's idea of how many think that economic progress for some comes only at the expense of others (McGhee front cover). This general concept articulated by author McGhee is called the zero-sum paradigm. The false notion is that the advantaged must retain benefits when the disadvantaged gain benefits.

Her question is, "why white people would view the presence of more people of color as a threat to their status?" (McGhee xix). She says that "progress for one group was an automatic threat to another...This zero-sum paradigm was...a framework for conservative media." All kinds of sayings are broadly circulated. For example, "They are coming for your jobs, safety, and your way of life" (McGhee xviii). By competition, each advantage for one group becomes a disadvantage for another (McGhee 388).

As an antidote for whites and the rest of us is profound. "We are greater than, and greater for, the sum of us." This would mean higher wages for the poor, enriched welfare programs, and better housing. In conclusion, McGhee affirms that there is power in the people. "We need to take this privilege that has come from exploitation of so many people, and that freedom, and create...the aspirations of tomorrow" (McGhee 287).

Questions

1. How do you see McGhee's ideas impacting your life?

2. Why do many experts understand McGhee's analysis of the zero-sum paradigm as a breakthrough in race relations?

What are the **cognitive** costs of privilege?

The costs or wastes from privilege are understood in terms of being a historic unmet opportunity. This type of waste means a loss of potential, exposure and recognition. Due to this kind of cost or waste from privilege, immense talent and creativity and dignity are held back and not permitted to strategically develop. It is like an untimely postponement, restricting powerful relationships, and thwarting of great ideas.

A young adult student told the author her response to just reading about privilege.

> I always thought of myself as a fairly open person...The reading went straight to my gut...It is extremely difficult to face the fact that what is given to us every day is something others don't have. We don't want to give it up...to share it. We all feel that we've paid the price in some way and deserve the right to have these privileges...I will begin to fight it...in whatever way I can (Student 1987).

Question

How possible is it for white students generally to fully understand their privilege and address it?

Dr. W.E.B. DuBois and Dr. Percy Julian

It took more than half a century for white scholars to discover and understand the broadened idea of white privilege as articulated by Black scholar Dr. W.E.B. DuBois. His views held that privilege was a fully human condition, not strictly an economic one. It was expected, therefore, that being white people conferred privilege that resulted in exploitation and alienation (Roediger 6, 12; Sehgal 12). Some fifty years after DuBois's important concept of privilege, Dr. Peggy McIntosh was awakened to its even wider reality – as discussed previously.

African-American chemist Dr. Percy Julian was blocked from academic/research efforts at Harvard and DePauw Universities, where he had previously earned degrees. So he acquired his PhD at the University of Vienna, Austria (Grose 1993, 2000).

Later Dr. Julian developed the synthesis process for cortisone so it could be mass-produced! The waste of respect, inclusiveness and time profoundly delayed the benefits of cortisone for all persons with arthritis and several other ailments (Julian 33). As stated in the slogan of the United Negro College Fund, "A mind is a terrible thing to waste" (UNCF).

Even for Christians, there is privilege. Evangelical pastor, Daniel Hill, forthrightly declared that the church has to "confront white privilege in Christianity, and create a multi-racial church. This could mean addressing its staff employment, rituals and issues and paying back to Indigenous people regarding land, and to Blacks various reparations" (McGhee 247).

Questions

1. What are a few ways that you can pinpoint the cognitive costs of privilege?

2. What do you think about the issue of waste?

Emotional costs of privilege

What are the **emotional** costs of privilege for parental fears and feeling inept as children?

We examine some emotional costs of privilege to us who are privileged, and then for us who are disadvantaged. The emotional costs of privilege seem subtle and harmless. Certainly, parents work to protect their children from harm, perceived and real.

Privileged parenting is firmly set in the dynamic U.S. society steeped in superior/inferior beliefs and hard-core stereotypes. When privileged parents protect their children, it partly means separating them from those who are culturally/racially different. Protection becomes almost synonymous with separation. Privileged separation is based on power (Jealous and Haskell 179).

Fear of intimate social relationships overruns parents' decision-making. They fear for themselves and their children. These emotions are re-enforced by beliefs from a superior/inferior social system. Privileged children's relationships out-of-school, for example, are often racially limited and intended to be superficial (Jealous and Haskell 20-22).

Privileged parents may imagine the worst possible will happen to their children when there is contact with kids of color – friendships and intimacy. Beyond that, they may fast forward to a specter of interracial marriage. This means that before long there will be mixed-race grandchildren! Some scholars suggest that this fear of interracial marriage is a single most important reason for a lack in progress in race relations (C. King 1990). Aren't there still occasions when adult children are still afraid to tell parents about "Guess Who's Coming to Dinner"?

Psychologist Caroline Haskell said, "I often reflect on how much I was deprived of as a child. To be one of privilege, ...you can imagine what I did not have the opportunity to experience. I still feel as if I'm in a catch-up course on life" (Jealous and Haskell 32).

Children of color are carefully educated by parents about the potential and actual harm when children are in stores, walking down the street, and associating with law enforcement. People of color educate their children about unearned disadvantage, not privilege.

Ann Todd Jealous has said that our teachers, counselors and parents have been unable to help with our childhood emotional situations. It "was largely a consequence of the lack of racial diversity in their own lives, and the ignorance and fear, that come from living with sameness" (Jealous and Haskell xviii). When placing our emotions within the framework of differences,

> it is neither necessary nor possible, unless one is blind or medically "colorblind," to miss color difference between people. What matters is what meaning we give to those differences. It is when those differences are tied to factors that determine success and failure...that they separate us from one another and create pain and hostility, fear and shame, guilt and grief (Jealous and Haskell 173).

Reflection. Exercise

Now, ponder how a variety of privileges can result in emotional costs for the disadvantaged. Then, review the succeeding list of items/emotions. You may talk with others regarding the emotional costs for those disadvantaged. Next, return to the entire list below and record information directly following as many of the items as possible. Using empathy and other approaches will be beneficial. Probe deeply and creatively.

Persons with unearned disadvantage feel

fear...

anxiety...

exhausted...

threatened...

hurt...

resentment...

inadequate...

humiliated...

inferior...

neglected...

helpless...

rejected...

anger...

desperation...

worthless...

hopeless...

powerless...

violated...

depressed...

grief...

Reflection

Ponder both your feelings and thoughts about addressing the emotional costs for those disadvantaged.

Wrap up with your story

Choose one of the following approaches in creating the story of our own privilege? You may choose to write a letter to yourself, develop a word picture, use "free verse" (not much punctuation), create a poem, compose a song, or paint a picture that clarifies your thoughts and feelings on privilege. This challenge only needs to be candid, understandable and to the point! One question is how can challenging privilege be worth it for ourselves and others?

Or for your story, journal your feelings and thoughts about privilege? Do you find changes in your approaches to privilege? Explain. And, to what extent are you motivated to do something about your relationship to privilege in daily life?

Concluding Actions

Take action <u>individually</u> by uprooting privilege

Journal or ponder any of the following questions.

1. What are a few conclusions you can draw about privilege?

2. What do your observations about privilege say about you as a person? How is it influencing your relationships? How is it affecting your self-understanding? How is it affecting your self-worth? What

might it take to dig more deeply into the subtleties and power of privilege?

3. Develop a blog statement, a poem or lyrics to a song on the topic "It is given to me."

4. Give one specific example of privilege, or its consequences, for each of the following categories: family, gender, sexual orientation, disability, religion, age, ethnicity/race, language and economic position.

5. "Power continues to be the determinant of privilege." Comment. (Lenski 56).

6. Raise at least two questions about privilege that still remain with you.

7. What else do you want to do about privilege?

8. Inform yourself in greater depth about privilege in articles/books on the subject.

9. What are the most valuable and the least valuable parts of this entire chapter on privilege? Explain why.

Dismantle privilege by taking action <u>with others</u>

The following questions and actions will chart still new territory <u>with others.</u>

1. Pursue how privilege presents itself, works/functions and is structured/set up in at least one organization. This might include learning more about how policies and rules are not followed, how power is shared and restricted, and/or how networking works at different levels in groups or institutions. All this means trying to get at what is hidden, behind the scenes. It is like investigating a mystery.

2. Privilege specifically points to issues of immense magnitude in higher education. And the focus on curriculum is a strategic key to revealing privilege. Course content is traditionally white and undermines the self-confidence of students of color and the knowledge base of everyone. White students have asked why colleges need courses and departments in Women's Studies, American Indian Studies and African American Studies. My response is, "Isn't this needed when the overall curriculum is white?" A further response is, "In addition to having strong

departments specializing in gender and race studies, we need to change the main curriculum to reflect everyone (McIntosh 2018).

3. With at least one other person, do a potential, or real experience where "I messages" are exchanged to illustrate the effects of privilege.

4. Discuss with a few others specific ways in which you could address privilege in everyday-life. Then try out any of these approaches in your social life, family, work, internet or with other relationships when different participants are ready. Preferably set a time and place when all of the participates can re-assemble to report on their earlier conversations.

5. Put up the privilege antennas in all kinds of situations. Intentionally converse with persons who appear to have different kinds of experiences with privilege from yours. The conversations with others may be a key to making progress in unmasking privilege. After building relationships, share stories of experiencing privilege. Even take leadership in discussing how groups can dismantle privilege. It may work to use a circle of interaction with all participants. Individuals tell their stories with privilege within a pre-arranged, equal time for each person.

6. Gather a few persons from different cultural backgrounds at an agreed-upon location. Discuss privilege/tell stories from each person's cultural perspective. (They do not speak for their culture or group.) Then brainstorm how cross-cultural coalitions might address institutional privilege.

7. Using the model of a game show, or a charades situation, present key points about privilege.

8. In a group/class, create a table game that illustrates/illuminates the effects of privilege and how privilege as a system works.

9. Select and read an item in the Works Cited section of this chapter and/or a book/article that directly discusses privilege. Share the resulting ideas with a few friends or relatives.

Works Cited

AMERICAN HERITAGE DICTIONARY. Houghton Mifflin, 2000.

Borgatta, Edgar and Marie (editors). ENCYCLOPEDIA OF SOCIOLOGY. Vol. 4. Macmillan, 1993.

Feagin, Joe and Vera Hernan. WHITE RACISM. Routledge, 1995, p. 21.

Goodman, Amy. "War and Peace Report." 10 Sep. Democracy Now, Free Speech TV.

Grose, Charles. Archives at DePauw University, Greencastle, Indiana, May 2000.

—, BLACK NEWSPAPERS IN TEXAS. Unpublished dissertation, University of Texas, Austin, 1972.

—, Interview with Anna Julian, Roosevelt University, Chicago, 29 Jan. 1993.

Hartmann, Thom. UNEQUAL PROTECTION. Berrett and Koehler Publishers, 2010.

Jealous, Ann and Christine Todd Haskell. COMBINED DIMENSIONS. Potomac Press, 2013, pp. 20-23, 32, 173, 179.

Johnson, Allan. POWER, PRIVILEGE AND DIFFERENCE. McGraw Hill, 2001, pp. 25-36, pp. 96-112.

"Julian Stamp Unveiled," JET MAGAZINE, 22 Feb. 1993, Vol. 83, No. 17, p. 33.

King, Charles. Guest on Donahue Show, WNBC, Oct. 1987.

Lenski, Gerhard. POWER AND PRIVILEGE: A THEORY OF SOCIAL STRATIFICATION. McGraw Hill, 1966, pp. 45, 56, 74-75.

McGhee, Heather. THE SUM OF US. One World, 2021, pp. xviii, xix, 247, 287, 388.

McIntosh, Peggy. Interview with the book's author, 28 Feb. 2018.

—, "White People Facing Race," St. Paul Foundations, 2009, pp. 6-7.

—, "White Privilege: An Account to Spend." St. Paul Foundation, 2009, pp. 2, 8.

—, "White Privilege: Unpacking the Invisible Knapsack." WOMEN'S INTERNATIONAL LEAGUE FOR PEACE AND FREEDOM. July/Aug. 1989, pp. 10-12.

National SEED Project, Wellesley College. Wellesley Centers for Women, 2018.

Newman, David. SOCIOLOGY. Pine Forge Press, 2008, pp. 291, 308.

NYT. "A Memorable Headline from the New York Times, April 16, 1912." 16 Apr. 2017, p. 2.

Pfarr, Jodi. THE URGENCY OF AWARENESS. MCP Books, 2019, p. 8.

RANDOM HOUSE DICTIONARY OF THE ENGLISH LANGUAGE. Random House, 1987.

Roediger, David. THE WAGES OF WHITENESS. Verso, 1999, pp. 6, 12.

Sehgal, Parul. "Power Play." NEW YORK TIMES MAGAZINE, 19 July. 2015, p. 12.

Schaefer, Richard. RACIAL AND ETHNIC GROUPS. Prentice Hall, 2010, pp. 116-118.

Student. Response to discussion in course names Educational Foundations. Minnesota: Mankato State University, Sep. 1987.

Thurman, Howard. JESUS AND THE DISINHERITED. Beacon Press, 1998.

UNCF.org.

United States, United States Bureau of Census, "Health Insurance in the United States," Government Printing Office, 2015.

United States, United States Department of Education. National Center for Educational Statistics, "Human Resources Survey, Academic Year 2013-2014, Government Printing Office, 2015.

Chapter 4

Is Talking about Race Still
a Discussion Topic?

Racism does not have to be experienced in person to affect our health. News coverage is likely to have similar effects. Studies have shown that when TV viewers observe scenes depicting racism, their blood pressure was elevated long after the scenes were over. It is reasonable to believe that when we see something we believe represents discrimination, our bodies pay a price, declared Dr. Douglas Jacobs a resident at Harvard Medical School (Jacobs SR3). Could that mean that undoing race enriches health?

Introduction

In relation to race, we pursue our vital journey with muted voices and loud outbursts that cling to uncharted experiences of being fearful and fearless, powerless and powerful, colorblind and colorful. You may reflect on a reasonable and resonating roadmap whose routes are relentless and resourceful. That roadmap results in resolved restrictions, respectful rewards, and restructured race relationships.

When boldly facing racial differences, we see that topics build upon each other and stimulate creative actions. Ethnocentrism, European colonialism, the myth of race, racial negatives, a theory of color-blind racism, broad inter-group relations, and reader's roles to confront racial inequalities unfold. Probing and comprehending race relations necessitates action. Exercises, role-playing, interviews, projects and closing queries mark those actions.

Conversations about race relations, and the simmering emotions behind them, often seem to result as a conversation stopper. An almost immediate result is to change the topic and maybe talk about a local sports team. Or a low-key response is "hmm" or "interesting." Many of us would call racial conversations an awkward or potentially explosive subject! In my case as a white male, I sometimes think about using a euphemism like ethnic relations, or people who are different, to possibly open some encouraging conversations.

Often when any of us face racial issues, fear inhibits progress. We, white males, are known to fear our ignorance/failure, our loss and being blamed. We do not want to hurt others or embarrass anyone, or say the wrong thing. We figure that something we say will be misunderstood and divisive.

Avoidance is not a viable focus and does not confront fears, ignorance and insecurities nor escape potential blame. Can challenging avoidance instigate productive relationships?

Any expected or unexpected change on our part can be perceived as threatening. We fear loss in power, prestige and privilege. Clinging to the status quo is a path of least resistance. Incorrectly, we may equate more equality for others with a loss for us. This is not the case. Because of actions based upon these previous insights and experiences, fear is likely to be allayed and/or eventually eliminated. Reciprocity brings positive power.

From those actions, we speak from a sense of responsibility and stronger feeling of security. All of this enhances self-esteem, status, and positive self-talk. When we feel secure, we need not put others down. We lift up others as we become mutually empowered.

Due to the length of **this chapter**, I suggest that **at least one break in the experience near the mid-way**. That could benefit individuals and groups who have a lot to digest with hands-on activity.

Exercise. Reflections to a question of discussing race relations

To be personal, here is a question for the head and heart. What comes to mind when you hear the words race relations? There are various ways in which you may deal with this open-ended question, including journaling. Brainstorming or divulging what's a gut response. Or become a storyteller about your race-relations experiences. Or initiate your thoughts and feelings around people of different cultural backgrounds, and related issues, experiences, etc. No response is wrong or right. Take your time and do not look for a long or short response. Just be candid, starting with yourself.

These reflections may, or may not, be given verbally and/or in writing to another person or in a group. Although opening them up to others often multiples the benefits on some occasions.

Operating mainly from the authority of one's personal experience is problematic.

There is danger in what I have presented at this point. And we may accept our individual experiences and ideas as the way it is in racial relationships broadly. We may not be aware of our short-sightedness or our experiential limitations. After all, they are so real to us. And that counts for so much. Dr. Charles King addresses these dilemmas within what he calls the "balance defense mechanism." In our thoughts and actions, we may use what we personally know to generalize or argue against what someone else says or experiences. So, we may present our perceptions to suggest that persons of color are negative or even positive, largely founded on what we think, feel and have experienced (King 1987). So common, tempting and human! Think about how limited is our experience contrasted to what else is beyond us, and all that we do not know about race relations.

Question

Think about a personal experience when you were tempted to generalize about a racial issue. It may relate to stereotyping.

What are some of the current, troublesome ideas and experiences that capture our attention about race relations in terms of...

Personal connections/interactions

Power issues

Mannerisms

Styles

Numbers in our population

Violence

Events

Killings, mass and individual

Families

Jobs

Government policies and laws

Religious

Authors

Music and art

Law enforcement

Values

Other items

Or you could journal and clarify your own list of detrimental racial "baggage" that is carried with you. That could be thoughts, feelings, habits, words, actions, and omissions?

Research

Who are some of your positive and inspirational persons of color? Research Google, other media experiences, books or articles. Ponder and include some journaling.

Pursuing Community Visits with People of Color

After the succeeding types of active learning experiences, journal a brief description of one experience below. Include your perceptions and insights from the events.

Select from and not be limited to the following:

1.   Festivals. A rich variety includes events of Indigenous "pow wows," Latino May 5 (Cinco de Mayo), Chinese New Year, Hmong New Year, Black musical programs, etc. Check the media for times and places.

2.   Religious experiences. Black Gospel Choirs, Black church services, Latino worship services, Buddhist meditations, Hindu Temples, Islamic mosques (not for worship).

3.   Community businesses. Restaurants, food stores, book stores, theaters, barber shops and salons.

4.   Racial Community centers. Latino/Hispanic, Indigenous, Chinatowns.

5.   Art and History Museums. Indigenous, Black, Asian, Latino.

Ethnocentrism Internationally

Isn't it valuable to explore big ideas behind the scenes? The time-honored concepts and experiences facilitate our deeper understanding, analyses and connections to racial relationships. Onward.

Meaning and examples

"My Country, Right or Wrong?" can lead us to the America first posture. This identifies ethnocentrism. Let's analyze ethnocentrism. Ethno refers to groups of numerous sizes. Centrism refers to being the center or focal point. This set of beliefs means that we see our group as the standard by which all others are judged.

Ethnocentrism is a viewpoint of ancient origin and very current usage. For example, 2500 years ago, people in "modern" China developed their own ethnocentrism by identifying themselves as the "Middle Kingdom." Even the Chinese language affirmed this concept through the meaning of the country's name China. The name China, Jungwo as used in Mandarin Chinese, translates into central kingdom. Other people were perceived as barbarians (Ocf Berkeley 1-3).

As recent as the early 1900s, the Hmong ethnic group in China was considered the Meo or barbarians partly because they had no written language at that time. The dispersed Hmong in Laos gave themselves their own name in the early 1900s which means free people (Grose 1981-1985).

Recent Chinese leaders, such as Hu Jintao, have spoken "admiringly of China as again the 'Middle Kingdom,' right under Heaven..." Currently, the expression of its fulfillment is the Communist Party (Young 1, 4). "The Communist Party believes its governance has restored China to its rightful position as the Middle Kingdom and is able to increase the country's position of respect globally...The concept of New China is synonymous with the Middle Kingdom (Watson 4-5). Why would China want to dismiss its ancient identification as the Middle Kingdom? It has a dominating population, land mass and political ambition.

In the powerful legacy of ethnocentrism, patriotic overseas Chinese in Singapore recognized the British as barbarians (Wong 53). A Chinese American who was born in Singapore said that he "learned to dislike the British and those who were friendly to them." Those of us from the West are identified by the Chinese as "red-hair devils" (Wong 70). As an actual U.S. redhead, I could be easily perceived as one of those devils.

Questions

1. What are current and personal examples of ethnocentrism? Be open, honest and do not hold back.

2. In what ways does ethnocentrism address standards or norms? Journal.

3. What is behind the view and action of ethnocentrism?

4. How can we illustrate the use of ethnocentrism in our country and even in small-scale groups?

Colonialism

From the oceanic forces of ethnocentrism stream the mighty waters of colonialism. Some of us became intrigued early in our education with the adventures of European explorers. We drew maps of the voyages led by what we thought were heroic figures. They drew out our curiosity, imagination and abilities to sketch world travels. Yet, we often did little to navigate the deep waters of colonialism until we studied British colonialism and our U.S. revolution against it.

The historic creation of European colonialism takes us to the early spread of Portuguese power and influence in the late 1400s. They were early shipbuilders. Among the other early European colonial powers were the Spanish, British, Dutch, Italians, French, Germans and Danish (O'Toole 2016).

Four interlocking dimensions of colonialism are economic exploitation, political control, military force, and zeal to convert the indigenous people to Western Civilization and Christianity (Feagin, RACIAL, 358). Generally, "colonialism means to be in charge of others, and structure indebtedness to the outside power" (Nelson 2015).

The concept of "cleanness of blood" emerged in the late 1400s with the Portuguese. "The filigree of blue-blood lies beneath pale skin was proof that one's birth had not been contaminated by a dark-skinned enemy"- initially meaning dark-skinned Italians and other Southern Europeans (Lacey 67).

At first, Africans were observed as a "spectacle of blackness" (Earle and Lowe 11). Overtime, they were defined as a subhuman, savage, and "other" because of their "different physical appearance and culture" (Cashmore 80). Consequently, "it was right for Europeans to capture and enslave black Africans…" (Earle and Lowe 11). A profound principle underlies our discussion of dominant-subordinate relationships. It is to define, then exploit. When people are defined as inferior, that becomes justification for exploiting them (Schaeffer 20).

It was the colonizer's duty to civilize the "other" (Singh 342; Cashmore 82). To be civilized was to be "Christian, rational, sexually controlled and white" (Feagin 358). This contributed to what Kipling meant by the "white man's burden" (Cashmore 81).

At the height of the slave trade in the 1700s, the English contended "that blacks…constituted property purchased from among prisoners of war and other prisoners in Africa" (Segal 43). In the American colonies, it was essential to become English. If "you already had white skin, you merely had to adopt the English language, worship within the Anglican Church, and profess loyalty to the British monarch…Yet skin color marked blacks as permanent strangers."

The militant Abolitionists of the U.S. North viewed slavery as an offense to fundamental moral law. Southerners saw slavery as necessary to establish equality and liberty for whites (Myrdal 87).

Beginning with the British in 1809, the Spanish and Portuguese officially ended slavery by 1823 (O'Toole 2015).

The United States became a colonial power after winning the Spanish-American War in 1898. The U.S. took control of the Philippines, Hawaii, Guam and Puerto Rico (O'Toole 2015).

I particularly felt my complicity in the colonial process and history after leaving Singapore. I was associated with power, money, status, suppression, opportunity, privilege, as an outsider. And I had the freedom to go home as needed during my four-year stay. I continued to understand that under the veneer of Western colonialism were deeply held and diverse Asian traditions.

Questions – Slaves are defined as property not as humans

1. On the international scene, what are current illustrations of colonialism?

2. What do you think it means when some insurance companies, churches and organizations still use the word colonial in their name or other names associated with colonialism? Explain.

3. What are some of the subtle and powerful vestiges of colonialism in the U.S. today?

4. Do you think that Indigenous reservations in the U.S. are structured remains of internal colonialism? Explain after yes or no.

Interviews. Interviewing persons who are racially different from the reader

So, let's engage others. This would mean that we interview at least three (3) persons from different groups as shown in each of the following categories: Asian Americans, Latinos/Hispanics, Blacks, Indigenous persons, and white Americans. Our purpose is to become more informed about various racial groups through the lens of individuals being interviewed. If they say that they are of mixed race, inquire about what they mean by mixed race. And, try to select and identify interviewees from different generations.

Arrange the interviews ahead of time. Tell the interviewees that these conversations will only take a few minutes in a relatively quiet location where neither of you likely will be interrupted. Inform them that cell phone calls can be answered after the interview, unless it appears to be an emergency. They will be honored to share something of themselves and especially their culture. Inform them to be candid and as specific as possible. Key points or a summary of each interview may be recorded in your journal.

As you start the actual interview, let them know that their names/identity will be held in confidence. Also, ask if they have any questions before you begin. This may help put them at ease.

Interview Questions

1. What do you see as a key reward about being a person of color or a white person?

2. What is a prominent hurt about being a minority person or a white person? (It is essential that each person answers from the perspective of being in a racial group!)

3. If the two main questions have not been answered to your satisfaction, you may want to inquire about what it means to be an American? Or where do you feel at home? With each question, it will be important to use follow-up questions to secure a more deep and specific response.

Post-interview question: how did their attitudes, information, and lives impact you? Try to be specific. Key points or a summary of each interview, and your post-Interview response, can be recorded in your journal.

Colorblindness

Presently, a dominant belief system that pervades our racial thinking and interactions is the idea of "colorblindness?" Dr. Charles King, Jr. asked a talk-show audience to think about these reactions. "I don't see color." "I'm colorblind to race." King said, "Wait a minute! When you say that you don't see color, it's like a man saying to a woman that you don't see her as a woman." How can that be true with women and people of color? To say that you are colorblind is to declare that you actually do see color (Charles King, Jr. 1987).

Color-blind racism is defined as the "use of race-neutral principles to defend the racially unequal status quo," said Dr. Richard Schaefer (Schaeffer 44). Colorblind racism is an ideological attempt to normalize inequality and diminish the lives and cultures of people of color while maintaining privilege, says Dr. Eduardo Silva (Silva 25-30).

Silva articulates that the "new powerful ideology of color-blind racism" is a type of "individualism, universalism, egalitarianism, ...and the belief that people and institutions can be improved" (Bonilla-Silva 25). When political actors applaud "individualism," they articulate the "bourgeoisie...middle class owner of property" (Bonilla-Silva 26-27).

In essence, individualistic choices reframe the meaning of ideas so as to obstruct the needs of the disadvantaged. We have heard the expression that a separate neighborhood "is the choice of the people, individuals." This ignores the institutional practices behind segregation and is insensitive to the negative consequences of the practices for minorities, according to Bonilla-Silva (Bonilla-Silva 28, 34).

"As colorblindness is most commonly practiced, it is...a silencer – a way of squashing questions about the continuing racial stratification in a society and a way of feeling good about the fact that the world of elites remains so predominately white" (Bonilla-Silva 124). As Ellis Cose inquires, "Are we at all serious when we talk about a society in which people are no longer judged by the color of their skin?" (Cose 209). And Silva states, "Whites cannot like or love persons they do not see or don't interact with" (Bonilla-Silva 124).

Bonilla Silva calls us to see ignorant views about people of color as a minimizing type of color-blind racism (Bonilla Silva 29). Minimizing suggests that discrimination is no longer a central factor in the lives of minorities." People say "It's better now than in the past" (Bonilla Silva 29).

Questions and Comments

1. Briefly comment on at least one idea about color blindness that you find to be important? Share that information with at least two others and ponder their feedback.

2. Why do you think that many persons say, "I don't see color?" Try to consider more than the views of the authors above.

3. Consider the complexity of the views about Black bodies and Black skin. "Black is beautiful," declared Stokely Carmichael in the 1960s (Grose). "In America, it is tradition to destroy the Black Body – it is heritage" (Ta-Nehisi Coates, 2015). Ta-Nehisi Coates' "mother knew... Perhaps it was the boys out there, who were black, telling her she was 'pretty for a dark-skin girl'" (Coates 2015). "Mankind is set free of the trampoline that is the resistance of others, and digging into its own flesh to find a meaning" (Fanon, 1967).

Colorism

How frequently do the variations in human skin color capture our attention? Our assessment of those different shades may result in a dynamic impact of discrimination.

We negatively perceive noticeable shades of skin color regarding whites, Blacks, Latinx, Indigenous persons and others. Whites have distinctive responses to the hues of skin color of people of color, and people of color see various responses to the distinctive color hues of themselves.

This negative personal experience is named colorism. Colorism means discrimination or prejudice, especially within a racial or ethnic group that favors people of light skin over those with dark skin (Meriam-Webster July, 2022).

Consider how social norms in society are connected to our issue of color. "If our social structures are embedded in notions of white racial supremacy, then anything that approximates that ideal norm is deemed more valuable," states professor Trina Jones of Duke University. There is less access to opportunities and rights due to darker skin tones, accompanied with curlier or kinky hair (Alfonseca 2021).

Latinos see that skin color is a discriminatory factor in getting ahead as well as shaping their daily experiences in the U.S. The impact of colorism is particularly prominent with dark-skinned Latinos. Overall, they receive less access to health care and gain lower levels of education among just a few types of experience (Pew, March, 2021).

Within racial groups, there are also traditional approaches to colorism. Even Latinos documented that they too experienced discrimination from someone who is Latino. Dark-skinned Latinos indicated that they were more likely to be treated unfairly by Latinos than those who were lighter in skin color (Pew March, 2021).

Among Blacks, I observed in their conversations and actions that showed their strong preference for light skin. Those experiences were found in a college, churches and informal gatherings (Grose 1967).

For all of us, it is crucial to be aware of and act on our contrasting choices between appreciating all shades of color and the discriminatory results of colorism. Rather than taking on the dominant culture's preference for lightness and whiteness, we can focus on the customs, art, music and other achievements of people of color. All these cultural influences are called socialization.

Questions

1. What have been your experiences with colorism? Remember the consequences of colorism.

2. As colorism is embedded in culture, what can you do to counteract the negative results of color evaluations? Journaling may bring up more in-depth clarity.

Discrimination

Broadly in relation to gender, sexual orientation, race and other negative designations, we implement detrimental acts. Biased opinions and prejudices may end up in discriminatory actions. Just as institutional policies and patterns may result in real-life discrimination.

Definition

Discrimination is the denial of equal rights and opportunities to individuals and groups for arbitrary reasons and feelings, determines Schaefer. (Gypsies, or the Roma in Europe, are still in North America and face discrimination) (Schaefer 60). From a group context, Feagin defines discrimination as "actions carried out by member of the dominant groups, or their representatives, that have differential and harmful impact on members of subordinate groups" (Feagin, RACIST, 16).

Questions

1. What do you understand as any basic differences between the definitions of discrimination by Schaefer and Feagin?

2. Why do you think the concept of discrimination is so important?

Race

Reality or Myth?

Humans have struggled with their differences from time immemorial. For our purposes, we will focus on the biological and social development of our attachment to the concept of race.

Strikingly the word race became clarified as it was connected to physical human appearance in the 1700s (O'Toole). Later, Euro-Americans and Europeans only used the word race with a distinct ranking system during the 1700s and 1800s. That stratification order from the highest to lowest included Caucasians (Europeans), followed by Mongolians (Asians), Ethiopians (Africans), Americans (Native Americans) and Malays (Polynesians). This system was created by a German anatomist, Johann Blumenback (Feagin, RACIAL, 4).

Believing in the old assumption that race was grounded in a biological category (Rex 75), human physical characteristics were considered hereditary. Biologists and physical anthropologists failed to base their conclusions on scientific observations but on prejudices and folk ideas of human differences (Feagin, RACIAL, 4).

So, how did the physical idea of race function? Persons who study animals and plants subdivided human beings into a so-called race based on characteristics like skin color, hair texture, head shape and transcendental essences. All this became a reason to divide humans on the basis of appearance for two centuries. For example, Blackness came from the vapors of the skin or darkened sperm. Heat and humidity from the tropics stained the skin. Add to that was the idea that the imagination of the pregnant mother imprinted her color onto her child (Gates and Curran SR7). European and U.S. scientists and writers were downgrading all people as "inferior" if they were not Northern Europeans by the late 1800s (Feagin, RACIAL, 4).

A part of this biological complexity was the creation of the infamous "one drop rule." Some courts called it the "traceable amount rule," and others named it the "one black ancestor rule." This meant that a single drop of "African blood" made a person Black. This whole understanding developed from the South and it became the country's definition. The "one drop rule" also affected Indigenous - white relationships (Johnson 6).

Many Blacks and whites have both European and African ancestry. Many "whites" are "Black" and most "Blacks" are "white." The main reason for this heritage is because of the thousands of circumstances in which white men raped Black women during the centuries of slave history and segregation (Feagin 200).

Then, by the mid-1800s, scientists concluded that the concept of biological determinism was erroneous. Currently, most scientists assert that we can no longer cling to the idea of biologically separate racial groups (O'Toole; Segal 44). The belief in innate white superiority is fictitious (Segal 43).

Can the understanding be that race can be a social invention? Can we affirm that the newer social invention behind the word race has become embedded in our minds and emotions? The social effect that membership has on persons identified with a particular race has on human interaction overwhelms the importance of race biologically (Schaefer 14). Consider what the UNESCO statement on race declares: "For all practical purposes, race is not so much a biological phenomenon as a social myth" (Montagu 118).

Recently, social scientists frequently call this social invention "The Social Construction of Race" (Schaefer 13; Feagin, Racial 4). "Races are distinctively meaningful because we attach meaning to them, and the consequences vary form prejudice and discrimination to slavery and genocide" (Bonilla-Silva, Re-Thinking, 472; Borgatta and Montgomery 2332). This social construction of race dictates that the "oppressor defines who is privileged and who is not... The acceptance of race allows racial hierarchies to emerge to the benefit of the dominant 'race'" (Schaefer 13).

From Gandhi's observations while living as a young lawyer in South Africa, he saw how "you could look on the exterior only. So long as the skin is white, it would not matter to you whether it conceals poison or nectar." That power of whiteness translated into discrimination against all nonwhites (Singh 343-345).

The tragic consequences of racial beliefs can be implemented by dominant-group policies and actions by a few power holders and their accomplices. Invented beliefs about different people being inferior has commonly produced intentional action toward vulnerable people and programed human slaughter.

Adolph Hitler manipulated the idea of the "Jewish race" and interpreted that issue into Nazi death camps. Contrarywise, Winston Churchill turned the idea of the "British race" to spur his people to fight Hitler. Both leaders used the word as a political tool. It is significant that in a "social setting that race is decisive" (Schaefer 14).

Race definitions became clarified in the concept of racial formation as described by Michael Omi and Howard Winant. Their process showed that racial categories are "created, inhibited, transformed and destroyed (Schaefer 13). The creation of Indigenous reservations in the 1800s is racial formation. This system about inferior races brought cleansing policies and practices to Indigenous people so that their children were programed to become white and Christian (Schaefer 14).

Are we ready to eliminate the myth of a human race? UNESCO, in 1978, reaffirmed the 1950 Declaration on Race and Racial Prejudice. It states that "All human beings belong to a single species and are descended from a common stock. They are born equal in dignity and rights, and all form an integral part of humanity" (United Nations 2021).

Twenty-first-century genetic technology has been able to determine individual origins. That new analysis promises to show that we have always been connected. Stories of our genes disclose "our ancestral diversity and under-score all that we – despite superficial physical differences – have in common" (Gates and Curran SR7). For example, Dr. Henry Louis Gates, Jr. discovered that his recent ancestral mutations trace back to his sub-Saharan and European roots (Gates and Curran SR7).

Add to my list of some racial words or expressions that were invented.

Whiteness and Blackness are simply a social myth (Gates and Curran SR7).

Race relations

Racial groups were created.

Human race

Questions

1. Why do you think that so many people hold on doggedly to the myth of race?

2. As a scholarly friend told me, "Why do you continue to teach about the false idea of race?"

3. What kinds of people care about the brutality that results from the racial myth?

4. Is it not our imagination whose open-heart still harbors the harm about race undenied and undone? Comment. (We imagine the potential actions and possibilities toward race and racism.)

5. What will it take to eliminate the myth of race? Look for imagination in your answer.

6. Since the idea of the human race was a human creation, where do you begin to uproot the myth of race?

Institutional Racism

Each day we are importantly involved in complex institutions to some degree whether we realize it or not. We are them and they are us! What we are referring to are schools, businesses, entertainment, communication, health care organizations, churches/synagogues/mosques and others. For our present attention to large-scale institutions, we particularly focus on the racial consequences of their operations.

Carmichael and Hamilton - Institutional Discrimination

A light switch was turned on when the light of institutional discrimination was brightly illuminated everywhere. Carmichael and Hamilton put an all-inclusive and clarifying focus on the acts of institutions within the phrase institutional discrimination. It describes colonialism, slavery, and the present-day inequalities within and among our political, economic, racial, educational, social, religious, gender, media, transportation, entertainment, military and health care experiences – in totality (Carmichael and Hamilton 4-6). In current parlance, institutional discrimination is understood as institutional racism (Grose). "Indeed, consensus is growing today that this institutional discrimination is more significant than acts committed by prejudiced individuals (Schaefer 63).

Unintentional and intentional institutional policies, programs and practices may profoundly result in excruciating problems, especially for persons outside institutions (Feagin, RACIAL 12). Among the endless examples of institutional challenge is this one about health, housing and government. "When there is arsenic in the water, 'we have nowhere to go.'" Residents reported ailments from rashes to cancer. Even though a state grant has been secured to build new affordable housing, the financial attempts to implement money have been slow and contentious. In one case of a mobile home park, the land is tribal and under the federal Bureau of Indian Affairs (B.I.A.). It has clarified that this complex issue has "multiple legal jurisdictions" and it is charged to enforce water standards. Yet, local leaders declare that the suitable "agency has not stepped up to help." Numerous mobile home parks have "their roots in the Bracero Program, which brought in Mexican" field workers during World War II (Facio-Krajcer and Cowan N13).

I was a staff person of a large institution that hired me to advocate in the community for a local Asian-American group. The vulnerable, new Asian-American group was being paternalistically treated and deprived of resources regularly available to white groups who were members of the large institution. Privately, I said to the institution's leader, "What we are doing differently to this (Asian-American) group smacks of racism" (Grose).

Questions

1. Illustrate what comes to mind when you identify institutions and systems that are racist. Explain what makes them that way? (Remember this includes practices and policies.)

2. When decades-long actions by realtors and banks guide persons of color through traditionally segregated housing policies, it is known as "redlining." Who can do something real about these old types of institutional actions today? Respond creatively.

3. In addition to my experience, what examples can you identify that show institutional exclusion as a form of racism?

"Reverse Racism"

"Reverse racism" is frequently misunderstood. Let us imagine that Asian Americans, Latinos, American Indians and Blacks are acting hurtfully toward others, and doing something "racist." That action alleges that people of color can be racists and take racist acts. Yet, racist acts depend on association to power. Since people of color are not associated with community power as whites are, then people of color cannot be racist. Only those of us in the dominant white group are associated with community power.

Therefore, to call a person of color a racist, it shows ignorance or a misunderstanding about power generally. It may just be a distraction. So let us stop using the demeaning term reverse racism. People of color, individually and in groups, are not associated with community power and are not racists. The key to grappling with racism is to consider it in terms of broad power within our society, and the policies and practices of institutions.

Exercise on Institutional Racism

As we work on the process of unlearning racism, it is crucial to experience it within our emotions. This means undoing racism within our personal lives and within institutions where we may wield power (McKinney 1994).

In the methodology of this group exercise, it is the learner who will experience a kind of disequilibrium. That personal involvement may be disquieting and may lead to growth. This becomes a wholistic approach that includes mind, emotions, senses and outside realities that may lead to transformation (McKinney 1994). Plan for an isolated place to do this exercise and allow for at least 30-45 minutes for the actions.

1. Ask a volunteer to leave the room and remain there so the volunteer cannot hear what is said in the other room.

2. Recruit five or six volunteers to stand and form a circle to create an "institution." Attempt to get at least one person of color in the institution. Then, name themselves as an institution.

    Give the circle institution these instructions: when the volunteer/outsider is invited back into the room, that person is not permitted to enter the institution under any circumstances. The outsider should experience the pain of exclusion.

3. Inform the outside that this is the _____institution. And the outsider must physically try to get into the institution. After unsuccessfully trying, the outside is told to sit down.

4. Next ask a person from the institution to leave and attempt getting into the institution. The circle will tighten up their institution and not permit the next volunteer to enter the circle. Let the new outsider sit down after they have tried to enter the circle with their best effort and not succeeded.

5. Now as the leader, you try to get into the circle. Declare that "I am going to enter this institution." If or when the institution does not let you get in, try to steal "junk" or a purse/wallet from anyone in the institution.

6. Thank the institution members and have them take their seats (McKinney 1994).

Discussion Questions from Leader

Take the time to process most of the succeeding questions. Those quires may not necessarily be followed in the presented order. Do all you can to keep persons from leaving the discussion because they did not like the experience. The experience may need a break.

1. Did anyone worry about a person's feelings?

2. Why did the outsiders try to physically attack the institution?

3. How did the outsider feel when they could not enter the circle/institution?

4. Who created the institution? What happened when the outsiders tried to enter the circle/institution?

5. Why did the institution presenters and outsiders follow the directions?

6. Do individuals lose their personal identity and feel compelled to conform?

7. Are people of color expected to hold the line so they will not lose their own positions in the institution?

8. Is it easier to hurt someone when you can't see them?

9. Does it take leadership (often from within) to make institutional change? (McKinney 1994).

Prejudice – two essentials, antipathy and stereotypes – Dr. Allport

Often linked to discrimination and racism is prejudice. Those connections can be clarified by the early work of psychologist Dr. Gordon Allport. Prejudice includes two essentials, a strong feeling of dislike and a stereotypical unfounded judgment.

First, prejudice is an

antipathy based upon a faulty or inflexible generalization. It may be directed toward a group as whole, or toward an individual because he is a member of that group...There are...references to unfounded judgment and to a feeling tone...A prejudice, unlike a simple misconception, is actively resistant to all evidence that would unseat it. We tend to grow emotional when a prejudice is threatened with contradiction" (Allport 6, 9).

We illustrate this strong feeling of dislike. Six months before the 2012 presidential election a retired Ohio State employee said in an informal discussion, "Certain precincts are not going to vote for Obama...I'll say it: it's because he is black" (NYT 1). This anti-Obama feeling was framed by his being black – his group association.

Questions

1. What makes prejudice so powerful?

2. What contributes to our discomfort in expressing our prejudices? You may need to journal a few examples which are meaningful for you and maybe others.

Second, Stereotyping – Walter Lippmann

How are stereotypes, the cognitive element of prejudice, fueling the engine of negative difference? Walter Lippmann, the journalist who coined the term stereotypes, suggested that for the most part "we do not first see and then define; we define first and then see...We pick out what our culture already defined for us." Stereotypes are "pieced together out of what others reported and we can imagine" (Lippmann VI).

For Lippmann, stereotypes enable us to economize our thinking and condense a great deal of information. They are mental pictures (Lippmann VI). "Stereotypes enable us to see a consistent picture of the world. We feel at home there. We fit in. We are members. And stereotypes are easily grasped representations, capable of condensing a great deal of complex information and host of connotations." Lippmann did not envision stereotypes pejoratively (Dyer 1999).

Defining Stereotypes Currently – illustrating its consequences

We presently define stereotypes as exaggerated generalizations that do not adequately consider the individual. How do stereotypes fuel the engine of negative difference? We vividly see a dramatic portrayal of stereotyping in the 2014 Ferguson, Missouri, tragedy. The killing of the unarmed, Black male teenager, Michael Brown, by a police officer in Ferguson, evoked massive, intense public protests. When citizens called the Ferguson Police Department hotline, they heard the protestors "being called monkeys and animals by dispatchers and the receptionist." The consequences of those stereotypes point to their power (Arnwine 2014).

In a commencement address, the president of the University of Akron in Ohio, spoke of stereotypes.

> These preconceptions are usually misconceptions, like blinders on a horse...They restrict our attention in ways that narrow our ability to see the important aspects of our environment...the whole picture... Even when not done maliciously, they can lead to the destructive process of ethnic/cultural profiling which is used to justify discrimination and persecution (Proenza 2003).

How can our personal prejudices not make a difference! In April, 2013, amateur investigators on Reddit (an electronic bulletin board) wrongly identified Boston Marathon crowd members as if they were bombing suspects. Their "online 'leads' were circulated to massive audiences on Reddit, 4Tran, Facebook and Twitter" (Kaufman 1). As a consequence, two innocent high school students fearing for their safety, were falsely accused (Lee 2013). In his apology, the general manager of Reddit said, "Activity on Reddit fueled online witch hunts and dangerous speculation that spiraled into very negative consequences for innocent parties" (Reddit is not news) (Kaufman 1).

Prejudicial "Baggage"

Journal a list of your prejudicial/stereotypical "baggage" you knowingly bring with you. That would include thoughts, feelings, habits, words, and even omissions. Be open, honest and do not hold back. When discussed in separate groups (female verses male, or people of color and whites), humor and enlightenment are almost always articulated.

Inter-Group Relations

Next, we address how inter-group relationships fit into our dealing with differences. Each day, don't we dance to the music of intergroup contacts? This means that powerful societal forces stimulate us to rhythmically shake or gracefully step to the tune of assimilation, cultural pluralism or a "melting pot" idea. We may not consciously recognize how we are influenced by these intergroup contacts and goals. Yet, these group goals (e.g., assimilation) tug and pull at us every day. In fact, cultural pluralism, "melting pot" and assimilation, as goals, actively and pervasively compete for our thoughts and actions. These goals will now be described and illustrated. More specifically we shall see and understand these intergroup goals through the lens of race relations.

"Melting Pot." In our media and our conversations, we so easily talk about any mixture of our groups, particularly racial interchanges, as a "melting pot" convergence of peoples. Almost a century ago, Zwingly wrote a play about the mixing of ethnic groups in the U.S. These groups were described as moving into a big pot where they were all "stirred up" and reshaped into a totally new identity as an American. Their previous ethnic characteristics and traditions were completely "melted" and no longer had meaning (Feagin, RACIAL, 346). Such loose descriptions of group interactions make it seem somewhat real, a mono-America. A basic formula for the "melting pot" would be A + B + C = D (Each letter representing a few of our many different groups) (Schaeffer 23).

Questions

1. How do you determine whether our ethnic/racial groups are moving toward a U.S. "melting Pot?"

2. Do you think the use of the "melting pot" idea distorts what is actually occurring today? Explain.

3. In what ways may each of us, and in our groups, help clarify the use and meaning of this community goal?

Cultural Pluralism. This inter-group relationship means that various groups share a mutual respect for each other's culture and expect their flexible group identities to continue. Yet, there remains an acceptance of some basic values, like the form of government and usually one core language. Persons of color expect to be treated without hostility A + B + C = A + B + C (Schaeffer 25).

Questions

1. Could the competition of racial groups likely result in one or more groups seeking cultural domination? Explain.

2. What actions may contribute to cooperation among those groups of color?

3. Some white individuals and groups fear that the numerical numbers of groups of color, and their potential political power, may result in people of color coalescing into the dominant power in society. Analyze whether you think that may happen. Journal.

Assimilation. All of us yield to the powerful customs, norms and rules of society. And when new people come into our communities and/or arrive from other countries, there is a magnetic draw for them to assimilate. In the United States, isn't it essential for people to learn the ways of our dominant culture to succeed? This means giving careful attention to the practices, traditions, values, institutions, and language of the U.S. dominant society/culture. A + B + C = A (Feagin, RACIAL, 26-33).

Questions

1. What are some of the pressures to make assimilation occur?

2. Does U.S. assimilation mean the process in which we have learned to experience whiteness?

3. Do you understand that to be an American is synonymous with our acceptance of dominant white culture?" Explain.

4. Based on our history's flushing out of our Indigenous children's culture in boarding schools, do you consider that such assimilation is a racist concept? Or because of that indigenous program, do you currently determine that it is an example of assimilation being racist? Journal.

Exercise. Which of the three models do you think is most appropriate for you, and for our society? Journal and illustrate how the goals of this three-point model could make a difference in your current activities. Among the areas you might address are language, customs, attire, norms/standards and practices.

Roles for Change

Germinating in the fertile ground of this chapter are the growing seeds of opportunity and change.

Just as the pollutants of oppression and discrimination compete for our future, so do the warm and enriching waters of personal action and commitment to fairness. Are we ready to talk about the racially different actions in our organizations and institutions? And do not our rallies, protests and conversations say that all of us are woven together in a tattered but repairable garment of mutuality?

What roles can you take to enhance racial relationships?

The succeeding thoughts translate into practical steps to improve race relations. Each step adds to a healthy process and a creative conclusion. Different roles you can pursue will be identified.

Starting with ourselves, we can recognize that we already have begun a healthy process while proceeding through this chapter. "Change is inevitable; growth is optional" reads the bumper sticker (Maxwell 245f).

Ally. This partnership includes persons and groups who substantially align with the cause and its methods as an ally. Broadly pursue and join a group in which you can participate in governmental actions. For example, ally with a group of color. Native Americans will be pleased that you did. "Indians practice generosity, and believe in sharing" (Zinn 7-8).

While teaching at a historically-white college, I became an ally of its students of color. I initiated and taught courses in their culture among traditionally white courses. Eventually, the students of color and a few of their allies became a catalyst for dramatic institutional change.

Questions

1. Currently, what can be done to partner with groups of color to bring social justice? (Black churches)

2. How might you volunteer for American Indian activities before Christmas or Thanksgiving with an Indian community center?

3. Could you join a local group of color or a national people of color organization? Comment.

Advocate. Individually, we can address the media and write letters to the editor. Consider speaking at or writing to any organization within an educational setting. Bolstering any issue collectively as an advocate is possible.

Indigenous photographer, Matika Wilbur, is capturing the identities and culture of all 562 tribes so we may change the way we see Indigenous Americans (Rivas 7). Latina poet, Ada Limon, engages the reader to feel the truth of who Indigenous people are and with whom we share the world. She is the National Poet Laurete for 2022-2023 (News 2022).

Questions

1. What online email note could you send about a crucial racial issue?

2. On any community issue, what letter to the editor might you develop?

3. What internet message about a racial issue could you send to racial organizations? e.g. UnidosUS – formerly National Council of La Raza, United Negro College Fund - UNCF, League of United Latin American Citizens - LULAC, Asian Americans Advancing Justice - AAJC), Assembly of First Nations - AFN, Canada.

4. Could you suggest exploring how more information about persons of color, and their ideas, could be included in a college's course curricula with social-science or humanities faculty?

Empathizer. Observe the effects of the killing of Ahmaud Arbery, who was jogging in a Georgia park, or any other unarmed Blacks who are constantly being killed by law enforcement. Starting with ourselves, we can recognize that we already have begun a healthy empathic process while proceeding through this chapter.

Questions and Comments

1. How could you empathize with Ahmaud Arbery's parents or relatives at Brunswick, Georgia?

2. In a personal letter to his parents, could you communicate the warmth of caring about them and the strength of sharing in their grief?

3. To a person of color, acquaintance, friend or organization, initiate a communication about a challenge they are given because of their racial identification.

Challenger. In so many cases in life, we are challenged by prejudices/stereotypes - discrimination and white nationalism. Bold are the intents and actions of everyday supremacists. This could mean photographing a crisis event.

As shown earlier, regular persons may harmfully act on prejudices and enable others to feel the brunt of those attitudes and stereotypes in daily experiences. "We need to hold stereotypes lightly and modify them gladly" (Lippmann VI).

From that backdrop of change and growth, we ask ourselves about how to challenge racist actions? Even individually, we can do what we alone decide. It may be a small act, but it is one more incremental step of progress.

Questions and Comments

1. Contact podcast initiators and other outside sources regarding racial concerns? Be creative. And we may raise questions and even confront our friends and relatives about racial issues. Of course, we may challenge ourselves about our own biases and questionable racial actions.

2. Can we also engage with a separate organization or coalition that is vigilant in challenging racial issues? Garner information from a national group which constantly addresses systemic racism?

3. Might we suggest to friends an article, online piece or a book that challenges racial actions?

Empowerer. A college student told this story. After years of hearing racist stories and remarks by an older relative, it was time to confront him. She told him that she could no longer be silent. She said that she did not agree with his views. Then, she bravely told him what she thought about other races and their actions (Grose 1988).

Keep aware that our critical thinking and growing understanding are complemented by our emotional power and empathy. Bill Holmes, a prominent-white thinker and leader, spoke with a room filled with persons at a Black college about his grappling with racism. He asserted that in his mind he believed that he was totally committed to racial equality. Yet, in his emotional heart of hearts, he often felt tendencies to diminish and exclude minorities (Grose 1967).

Questions

1. What are positive actions that may empower you to stand up and speak out on racial experiences?

2. What are a few of the countless ways we can share in empowerment by recognizing our positive decision-making on race?

3. Do we experience the contradiction of positive thoughts and negative emotions about people of color? Explain.

Activist. Naturally, our activist role is broad and inclusive of other roles. We can be inspired to figure out our own roles by connecting with superstar Alicia Keys. She

> wants to work with you fans at the grassroots level. Many...feel helpless to make a difference...How can we take the next step...as opposed to just being angry?...The next steps... will include petitions, rallies, protests and public awareness efforts, as well as fundraising... She will encourage her fans to support specific groups...She aspires to be a moral voice as well as a musical one (Kristof 11).

The mystery of Paulo Freire's succeeding words may offer an explanation to the paradoxical relationship between the oppressed and the oppressor. "It is only the oppressed who, by freeing themselves, can free their oppressors" (Freire 38). The oppressed know the weaknesses of the oppressor who believe "To be is to have...Others are things... (Freire 57).

"The only effective instrument in this humanizing pedagogy is a permanent dialogue" among the oppressor and the oppressed (Freire 66). Pedagogical action can transform the dependence of the oppressed into independence (Freire 68).

Questions

1. What may motivate us to be a short-term activist?

2. What may pull us to take an activist role for a specific purpose?

3. Why do some persons become life-long activists? What may be behind that commitment?

4. What difference does a small group of personal associates make to a life-time activist commitment?

Exercise and Reviewing the Reader's Choice of Roles

Now it is your time to be empowered by your experience with roles. First, you may want to pinpoint a particular situation to which you can address your personal roles. Or, you may desire to prioritize the roles that fit for you. Still further, you may just begin by choosing a few roles that may be generally enriching for you. Following that, journal how you could use those roles in a real-life circumstance.

Overcoming the Power of Racial Privilege

We accept that much of our distinctive power derives from racial privilege. And when we defy the power of that racial privilege, we are lifted up to be our better selves.

Instead of feeling guilt, we can feel healing,

estrangement, we can feel inclusion,

emptiness, we can feel fulfilled,

ignorance, we can feel affirmed,

fear, we can feel free.

Conclusion

We have challenged race and its coordinated ideas without being overwhelmed. Many persons only connect with the racism of the violent white nationalists or the blatantly bigoted lives of everyday Americans. Our viewpoints also may include the innocent and those who unknowingly commit racial acts or avoid standing up to racial oppression.

The magnitude of our racial commitments requires prioritizing our singular efforts. As we travel this terrain, may our role modeling wake up the speechless to bold words and brave actions. All this means we may earn real solidarity with persons who are racially different.

Wrap up your Story, and Questions

Identify and journal your thoughts about race relations as a part of your story from this chapter.

Journal your feelings about your experiences with this chapter.

Record feelings and thoughts from this chapter which may have changed over your attention to this chapter.

From this heavy-duty chapter, consider how that experience connects with your everyday life.

Questions

1. Do you agree or disagree that race relations are improving in the U.S.? Explain.

2. With the magnitude of our needs, how may we prioritize our energies and time to include racial issues?

3. Zimmerman's killing of Black Travon Martin is not simply the "product of a sick mind but of a sick society. This excuses nothing that Zimmerman did as an individual, but it finds a more substantial explanation for his actions in a defective pattern rather than a defective personality" (Younge, 11). Specifically comment on this commentary.

4. Robert Lockhart, an Indiana University professor, says that he was "growing up in a culture that discriminates against people who are different, and what was most troubling for him was that he was vitally complicit in this discrimination." Discuss this issue of complicity from within a discriminating culture. Do you hold similar views with Lockhart or not? Explain (Lockhart 5).

Works Cited

Allport, Gordon. THE NATURE OF PREJUDICE. Addison-Wesley Press, 1989, pp. 6-9.

Arnwine, Barbara. "The Morning Joe Show." MSNBC TV, 20 Aug. 2014.

Borgatta, Edgar and Rhoda Montgomery. ENCYCLOPEDIA OF SOCIOLOGY. 2nd Edition, Vol 4, Macmillan, 2000, p. 2331.

Carmichael, Stokely and Charles Hamilton. BLACK POWER. Random House, 1967.

Coates, Ta-Nehisi. BETWEEN THE WORLD AND ME. New York, Spiegel and Grau, 2015, p. 103.

Cose, Ellis. COLORBLIND. Harper Collins, 1997.

Dyer, Richard. "The Role of Stereotypes" in Morris, Paul and Sue Thornham. MEDIA STUDIES: READER. Edinburg University Press, 1999, para 1-3.

Earle, T.F. and K.J.P. Lowe (editors). BLACK AFRICANS IN RENAISSANCE EUROPE. Cambridge University Press, 2005.

Facio-Krajcer, Ana and Jill Cowan. "When There's Arsenic in the Water, But 'We have Nowhere to Go.'" NYT, 31 July 2022, p. 13.

Fanon, Franz. BLACK SKIN, WHITE MASKS. New York, Grove Press, 1967, p. 9.

Feagin, Joe. RACIAL AND ETHNIC RELATIONS. Prentice Hall, 2003, pp. 2, 4, 12, 16.

—, RACIST AMERICA. Routledge, 2000, p. 5.

—, WHITE RACISM. Routledge, 1995, pp. 25-33, 40-43.

Freire, Paulo. PEDEGOGY OF THE OPPRESSED. Continuum, 1970, pp. 31, 34, 38, 51, 55-57, 65-68.

Grose, Charles. Statement by a white student in a minority studies class. Mankato State University, Minnesota, Fall Semester, 1988.

—, Work with Hmong refugees. St. Paul, 1981-1985.

Holland, Jessica and Kimberly Hefling. "Report: School Integration Slipping 60 Years After Brown." ST. PAUL PIONEER PRESS, 15 May 2014, p. 16A. https://www.meriam-webster.com/dictionary/colorism

Jacobs, Douglas. "We're Sick of Racism, Literally." NYT, 11 Nov. 2017, SR7.

Johnson, Elizabeth. "One-Drop-Rule and Amalgamation: 1770-1860." Thesis, Mankato State University, May 1999, p. 6.

Kaufman, Leslie. "Bombings Trip Up Reddit: Its Turn in the Spotlight." NYT, 28 Apr. 2013, p. 1.

King, Dr. Charles. Interview on the Phil Donahue Show. NBC TV, Oct. 1987.

Kristof, Nicholas. "Alicia Keys Asks: Why Are We Here?" NYT, 21 Sep. 2014, p. SR11.

Lacey, Robert. ARISTOCRATS. Little Brown and Co., 1983.

Lee, David. "Boston Bombing: How Internet Detectives Got It Very Wrong. "BBC NEWS, 19 Apr. 2013.

Lippmann, Walter. PUBLIC OPINION. Free Press, 1922, Chapter VI.

Lockhart, Robert. "Confessions of a White Bigot," paper delivered at the Fourth Annual Pedagogy of the Theater and the Oppressed Conference, Omaha, NE, 5 Mar. 1998, p. 5.

Macionis, John. SOCIETY. Prentice Hall, 2002.

Maxwell, John C. THE 21 IRREFUTABLE LAWS OF LEADERSHIP: FOLLOW THEM AND PEOPLE WILL FOLLOW YOU. Thomas Nelson, 10th edition, 2007, pp. 245f.

McKinney, Karen. "The Road to Understanding." Paper in Ethnic Studies, Mankato State University, MN, 1 Dec. 1994.

Mitchell, Andrea. "Andrea Mitchell Show." MSNBC, 26 June 2022.

Myrdal, Gunnar. AN AMERICAN DILEMMA. Harper & Row, Vol 1, 1962, p. 87.

Nelson, Dr. Chuck. Interview with sociologist on colonialism. Minneapolis, 15 June 2016.

NEW YORK TIMES, 11 May. 2012, p. 1.

News Release. Library of Congress. "Ada Limon is the 24th Poet Laurette Consultant in Poetry," 2022-2023, 12 June. 2022.

Noe-Bustamante, Luis and Ana Gonzalez-Berrera, Khadijah Edwards, Lauren Mora, and Mark Hugo Lopez. "Majority of Latinos Say Skin Color Impacts Opportunity in America and Shapes Daily Life." PEW RESEARCH CENTER, Report, 4 Nov. 2021.

Ocf.berkle.edu "World Civilizations: China." pp. 1-3.

O'Toole, Dr. Tom. University professor, Lectures on European Colonialism and Beyond. Apr-May. 2016, Minneapolis.

Proenza, Luis. Commencement Address. University of Akron, Ohio, 13 Dec. 2003.

Rex, John. COLONIALISM AND THE CITY. Routledge, 1973, p. 75.

Rivas, Josue. "Through a Lens: A Documentary of Indigenous Culture." NYT, 18 May. 2022.

Schaeffer, Richard. RACIAL AND ETHNIC GROUPS. Pearson Inc., 2010, pp. 20f.

Segal, Ronald. BLACK DIASPORA. Macmillan, 1996, pp. 13, 34, 43-44.

Silva, Eduardo Bonilla. RACISM WITHOUT RACISTS. Rowman and Littlefield, 2003, pp. 24-30, 124, 134, 144.

—, "Re-Thinking Racism." AMERICAN SOCIOLOGICAL REVIEW. Vol 62, No 3, June. 1997, p. 472.

Singh, Hira. CONFRONTING COLONIALISM AND RACISM. Schumer, 2007.

Tavernise, Sabrina and Jeff Zeleny. "In Ohio, Hurdles for Both Candidates." NYT, 19 Apr. 2012, p. A1.

Watson, James. CLASS AND SOCIAL STRATIFICATION IN POST-REVOLUTION CHINA. Cambridge University Press. 1984, pp. 4, 5.

Winfield, Nicole. "Francis Comes to Canada to Apologize for Church Schools." NYT, 24 June. 2022, p. A2.

Wong, Samuel. A CHINESE FROM SINGAPORE. Xlibris Corporation, 2009, p. 53.

Young, Stephen. "The Danger in Perceptions of Destiny." op ed. STAR TRIBUNE. 18 Apr. 2014, pp. 1, 4.

Younge, Gary. "The Awkward Truth About Race." THE NATION. 9/16 June. 2014, p. 10.

Zinn, Howard. PEOPLE'S HISTORY OF THE UNITED STATES. Harper, 2003, pp. 7-8.

Chapter 5

Everyday Violence and Its Alternatives

A self-proclaimed addict throws a night clerk to the floor, sits across her chest and holds a knife to her throat. At that time, she recalled her training in nonviolence from Dr. Rosenberg. He had said, "Never put your 'but' in the face of an angry person." She was about to say, "BUT I don't have a room." She didn't. "The more I was able to focus my attention on his feelings and needs, the more I saw him as a person full of despair whose needs were not being met." After 35 minutes of deep breaths, a lot of listening and empathizing, he released her and she talked with him about lodging at another facility (Rosenberg 125-126).

"What I want in my life is compassion, a flow between myself and others based on a mutual giving from the heart," affirmed Marshall Rosenberg (Rosenberg 1).

Introduction

The prominence of justice and change run throughout the issues of violence and nonviolence in this chapter. Dr. Martin Luther King, Jr. and Gandhi practiced nonviolence in their everyday life.

The pervasiveness of naked violence can hardly be doubted in our current world, let alone under-the-radar-subtle violence. We do not need to accept the inevitability of violence nor its unchangeable condition. In this chapter, we selectively focus on American Indians, lynching, law enforcement and black men, bullying, violent extremists, gun violence in schools, recent student activism, institutional policies that injure the vulnerable, and what can be resolved. These critical issues are largely chosen because of their contemporary appropriateness for the timeless significance of corresponding problems.

What can be done with nonviolence is highlighted. The raw edges of violence cut deeply and pervasively into necessary antidotes.

Gandhi and Nonviolence

Imperative to our introductory study of nonviolence are the vital principles and practices of Mohandas Gandhi. The essence of nonviolence is framed as truth in action combined with respectful behavior. Gandhi's nonviolence became strategic in winning independence for India.

Through his mix of introspection and activism Gandhi's evolution to nonviolence was undergirded by Hindu spirituality (Fischer 87). He integrated ahimsa (do no harm) with his newly formed terminology satyagrapha (truth force). Truth implies love and satyagrapha means "firmness in a good cause" or "soul force" (Gandhi 504-505).

Gandhi's professional, economic and political capabilities "were gradually consolidated into an overall identity of service" (Erikson 196-198). The campaigns for justice in South Africa became identified as satyagraphi as were his highly trained volunteer activists (Gandhi 407).

Whether the challenging circumstances were interpersonal, e.g., against a home robber, or institutional, or against apartheid laws, Gandhi became an icon in addressing violence. Sometimes known as a "conscience in action," Gandhi said that a person "should not do what he knows is wrong and suffer the consequence whatever it may be. This is the key to the use of "soul force" (Erikson 225).

Exercise

Nonviolence and Gandhi's spirituality can be understood while completing the following phrases: his

Principles are...

Methods are...

Dr. M. L. King, Jr. and Coretta Scott King and Non-Violence

Dr. King articulated and lived by his profound system of non-violence. His principles pick our minds and actions for inspired grappling with everyday life.

1. Non-violence is a way of life for courageous people. It is active non-violent resistance to evil.

2. Non-violence seeks to win friendship and understanding. The end result of non-violence is redemption and reconciliation.

3. Non-violence seeks to defeat injustice, not people. Evildoers are victims and not evil people.

4. Non-violence holds that suffering can educate and transform. Unarmed suffering is redemptive.

5. Non-violence choses to love and not hate. It resists violence of the spirit as well as the body.

6. Non-violence believes that the universe is on the side of justice. God is the God of justice.

It is a guide for social and inter-personal change (King Center 2015).

Exercise

The epitome of King's beliefs and actions now challenge us to use his principles. Journal your personal response in a paragraph about non-violence. You may wish to address your ideas by utilizing the following word scramble, and taking any other words that express your thinking about non-violence.

confident	trust	doubt	fear	hope	acceptance
rejection	risk	courage	indecisive	committed	
overwhelmed	inadequate	withhold	belong		
separate	persevere	insecure	idealistic		

What is the most accepted religion in the world? Many believe it to be violence. Several episodes in the chapter illustrate vital connections between violence and race. While this is heavy lifting involvement, the reader also is enticed to offer areas of hope and resolution.

Mass gun violence by three old Asian men struck the Asian communities of Los Angeles and Northern California's placid Half Moon Bay in January, 2023. Mr. Chou, Mr. Tran and Mr. Zhao committed their shootings "not because they were Asian but as Americans. Mass murder may be the fullest act of assimilation possible into a culture that has proudly chosen as its colors the red of innocent blood, the white of panicked eyes, and the hazy blue of semiautomatic smoke" (Yang SR7). Most violence is toward persons and groups of color by outsiders. This information vividly sets the stage for racial violence in 2023.

Do you believe, or not affirm, that violence is the main religion in the U.S.? Explain.

How broad are the subsequent unnoticed acts of violence?

In Coretta Scott King's 1969 speech only a few months after Dr. King's assassination, she asserted that often hidden conditions are acts of violence. In what ways are these violent acts?

Is neglecting school children of color? Briefly respond.

Is ghetto housing an act of violence? Briefly discuss.

Is ignoring the medical needs of people of color an act of violence? Briefly discuss.

Is indecision about the needs of people of color an act of violence? Briefly discuss. (Blow 10).

White and Black styles of communication add another dimension to violent conflict. For example,

> when opponents become angry and engage in verbal dispute, whites feel that they are reducing the danger of violence by keeping the antagonists apart...Public argument, if not stopped, will inevitably escalate into violence. Blacks believe that personal differences can only be worked out by engaging in the struggle...Blacks believe in...the possibility of reconciling differences... Consequently, Blacks conceive the danger of violence as greater when people are not communicating with each other (Kochman 58).

Question

What do you think is behind the differences between verbal Black and white communication?

American Indians

Too often people only single out Dakota life in relation to the War of 1862, declared Minnesota Poet Laureate Dr. Gwen Westerman. "There is more to Dakota history than December 26, 1862," the date of the mass execution of 38 Dakota Sioux in Mankato, Minnesota. And there are more than two sides of this story." - Dakota and white settlers (Tongas 19). That lynching was ordered by President Lincoln after he had pardoned many other Dakota. And for that hanging, American Indians do not think highly of Lincoln.

Another solution to organizational exclusion of Indigenous people was for them to build their own group. A national literacy society refused to select a single leader of its society from its American Indian members over many years. Westerman, and other Indigenous members, finally left their longstanding association and started their own Native American Literature Symposium, NALS, in 2002. They said that Native worldviews can be expressed and considered in all variations...We can stand on the shoulders of incredibly strong Indigenous people...We remember that walls not only shut others out but also shut us off from others...We continue to travel on routes that were laid out generations ago as we share our stories (Westerman 2017).

Question

What questions can you the reader pose about any of Westerman's previous information?

Strikingly, non-Indian perpetrators constitute 96% of violence against Indigenous women (WH.Gov 22). President Biden signed into law the 2022 Violence Against Women Act, VAWA, a Congressional bipartisan legislation. The law seeks to "address the epidemic of missing or murdered Indigenous people...It disproportionately affects Native women and girls." Strengthening the original law, the new law includes "expanding special criminal jurisdiction of Tribal Courts to cover non-Native perpetrators of sexual assault, child abuse, stalking, sex trafficking, and assaults with Tribal law enforcement officers on Tribal lands (WH.Gov 2022).

In the four situations below, journal how the women might be vulnerable to outside violators.

Non-Indian perpetrators can accost urban women in and around Indian businesses and housing areas.

Consider how casual contacts from weekly bingo events on the reservation may result in violence.

Informal relationships with tribal-women employees in reservation motels and casinos also may help initiate convenient venues for violence.

And, perpetrators may be driving through a reservation and use guns and/or deceptive persuasion as in drug opportunities which may result in violent acts.

"Native women will not be vanquished. In the words of a Cheyenne proverb: A nation is not conquered until the hearts of the women are on the ground" (Katz 6). There is reason for hope because the hearts of Indigenous women are not on the ground.

Anti-Lynching and Black Americans

Consider the line in the speech of Justice Kenanji Brown Jackson regarding her approval to be the first Black woman in the U.S. Supreme Court. She declared, "I am the dream and the hope of slaves (MPT Daily 2022).

Comment

Comment on Justice Brown Jackson's line in her speech. (You may note her becoming the Black Justice and the dream of slaves.)

Lynching and Anti-Lynching

After a century of over 200 attempts, an anti-lynching bill was passed by Congress and signed by President Biden in 2022. Previously, our legal/political system was the primary obstacle to protecting citizens of color. Southern Republican lawmakers in Congress and in the Democratic Party had "acted as a bloc." (Bouie 9).

Lynching is more than a violent act meant for a single individual. Past and present, lynchings are meant to intimidate an entire community," said Vice President Kamala Harris at the passing of the Anti-Lynching Act. Author and historian Amy Louise Wood explains in her book that "lynching had a singular psychological force generating a level of fear and horror that overwhelmed all other forms of violence" (Bouie 9).

Questions

1. Why do you think that congressional Southern Elites had an unbreakable veto power in the politics of the region for so long? Try to be concrete in your answer.

2. What do you think contributed finally to getting the law passed?

Author and lawyer Bryan Stevenson helped create the idea of the intriguing National Peace and Justice Museum in Montgomery, Alabama. It is dedicated to the victims of white supremacy. Would you believe that over 4,400 known Black persons died from lynching? Stevenson said, "I believe that each of us is more than the worst thing he has ever done...I have to believe that for everybody. I am not interested in talking about American history because I want to punish Americans...I want to liberate Americans..." (Robertson 14).

Questions

1. Having read about the museum, what are your initial thoughts about it?

2. What gut feelings do you have about lynched Black men from the museum experience?

3. What do you think Stevenson means when speaking about "liberating Americans?"

4. What thoughts do you have about placing the names of lynched Black persons on the steel columns of the museum?

5. What deep emotions may you experience around the anti-lynching museum? At least, journal this last question.

Black Men, Women, Youth and Law Enforcement

Our lens now may be framed on the issue of "race" and the vulnerability of Black bodies. The bodies were "exploited through slavery and segregation, and today threatened, locked up, and murdered out of all proportion. What is it like to inhabit a black body and find a way to live with it?" (Editors, book cover). It is racism that "ascribes bone-deep features to people and then humiliate, reduce and destroy them…" (Coates 7).

Journal some of our feeling and thoughts about living within Black bodies.

The piercing, painful patterns of hands-on (handgun) killings of Black men by police dominated our media attention since Travon Martin's death in 2012 at Stanton, Florida. A treacherous, terrifying trail of the killing and destroyed relationships of unarmed Black males zigzags from Florida to Wisconsin and beyond. Cell phone videos, police cameras, and mainstream media put the unprecedented tragedies into our faces! Among the other highly publicized, unarmed Black males who have been killed by police are Tamir Rice (Cleveland), Eric Gardner (New York), Michael Brown (Ferguson), Freddie Gray (Baltimore) and Tony Robinson (Madison) (Fulton and Martin 2017). Also, a tremendous impact has been shown by the murder of George Floyd (Minneapolis) in the MINNEAPOLIS STAR TRIBUNE, and national and international media.

Themes Surrounding Law Enforcement and Death of Black Men and Women

Heart-wrenching themes run through the data on police violence against unarmed black males killed by racial-profiling law enforcement. They are rarely indicted. Often the only accountability comes from photographs by innocent bystanders in the daylight of urban neighborhoods. And, the grieving parents of victims often establish conciliatory programs and foundations to improve gun-violence education.

Question

What empathy can we show about any or all the above themes?

Community responses to killing of Black men by law enforcement

Racially diverse, mostly peaceful protests immediately follow the killings of Blacks near the death sites and nationwide. Media coverage sensationalizes property damage, e.g., fires by rioters, and presents interviews of persons close to the incident. A problem of Black males 16-24, ranging from 12 percent to 28 percent, survive on crime and underground illicit trade. Precautionary safety advice from Black parents, and white parents of Black sons, is mirrored by community acts of Black sons and daughters. The bigger picture of urban racial violence is understood as a concentration of poverty, a culture of violence among a small minority (especially young males), and "out-of-control law-enforcement practices" that "prioritize racial profiling" (Patterson SR6).

Law enforcement can act differently because

social workers can first face complicated issues at houses and...

de-escalating action can be done at the local conflict scene through...

law enforcement can change their mindset from warrior to guardian as they...

law enforcement can prioritize protection rather than investigation in communities by...

law enforcement may develop a new police culture by...

Provide an example of how two of the above actions might be enacted.

Coalitions intertwining comprehensively to support justice

A community/citizens review board can do more than be a law enforcement watchdog. Subpoena power of some kind will strengthen the board's power to bring peace officers to increased accountability. The board could include barbers/beauty stylists, coaches, rappers, social workers, school nurses, small-business persons, religious representatives, high-school and college student leaders, and youth who are respected Twitter communicators. Various ethnic and racial representation will provide added validation.

Local community partnerships and coalitions with local organizations provide immense assets for developing critical relationships and multiple opportunities. Mutual engagement among local businesses, gangs, religious groups, housing organizations, law enforcement, community organizers and others need to be intentionally addressed (Sharrow 1).

Finally, a few intertwined approaches can make a practical difference for low-income boys of color and men facing violence and its repercussions. A re-vamped sentencing system for nonviolent crimes will keep males out of prison or have reduced confinement. With at least a $15 minimum wage, and an eradicated stigma for previously incarcerated inmates, parents can more likely provide for their families. This implies a reduction in the number (72%) of children born to single parents, often poor women. Consequentially, this would mean less risk of child abuse, youth delinquency and violence (Sharrow 1).

Question

What is it that makes the killing of Black persons so tragically compelling? Journal.

Black Youth - "Pipeline from school to prison"

Powerful arenas commonly influence youth of color – home, school, church, gangs and prison.

The intersecting policies that push kids from school into a punitive legal system are known as the "school to prison pipeline." Correctional institutions must be challenged to take a child's education seriously, including high expectations (Knefel 22, 24). Even 12-year-olds "who get into trouble with the juvenile justice system often never complete a school year as a free child again." Key policies have kept young persons in poverty from completing their education: high-stakes testing and high-stakes discipline (Knefel 23).

And youth may be placed in special education classes where they could feel that something was deficient about them. Frequently the students were behind in credits from classes missed while in custody. And a school can refuse to re-enroll those students. When the juvenile justice system is in charge, the schools did not make the inmate students a top priority. And when school districts are in charge, the superintendents often are too busy to invest in the former inmates (Knefel 22). If a student is arrested for gun possession at school, he/she could spend time in nonsecure and secure juvenile facilities (Knefel 23).

The "main reason for joining gangs is to find a family and a male role model." One gang member said, "I grew up looking for somebody to love me in the streets. You know, my mother was always working, my father used to be doing his thing. So, I was by myself...I ain't got nobody to give me love, so I went to the streets to find love" (Patterson SR6).

To counteract the rigidity of semester systems, David Domenici of the Washington, D.C., school system, has created an academic year broken into 22-day units. This way, the students are more likely to complete their credits in a curriculum organized around themes (Knefel, 20, 23, 24).

Question and Role Playing

What measures need to be taken to specifically eliminate the school-to-prison pipeline? Journal. Or, individual readers may imagine they are participants (role players) in the" pipeline" process. Thinking/talking about the roles, or journaling them, individuals may play the role of student, peers, teacher, juvenile-system judge, or a prison authority. When a group role plays, it will include what was addressed for each individual. And a new, separate group can roleplay a different perspective on the whole experience.

Gunning - Children and Youth

Gunning is among the multitude of experiences in which children and young people are currently violated in the United States. At least a generation ago, many of the high-profile shooting sprees were conducted by teenage boys. Shockingly two Columbine High School students, in Littleton, Colorado, killed twelve fellow students, one teacher and themselves in 1999. In addition, Sandy Hook Elementary School, in Newtown, Connecticut, Virginia Tech University, in Charlottesville, Virginia, and the University of California, in Santa Barbara, made national media headlines for massacres by guns (Carter 135-140). "More than 187,000 students have been exposed to school shootings since Columbine in April 1999" (Williams 11).

Each deadly eruption perpetuates its own fiendish emotional, intellectual and physical loss, cost and trauma. These deliberate acts of gun violence in schools only begin to identify the other gun deaths in churches, temples, mosques, entertainment area and more.

Currently, among mass murders, "mental illness is not a useful means to predict gun violence." Rather, it is a "life crisis that is the predictor of violence" (O'Hare 7). Other related factors include "extreme feelings of anger, social alienation, ruminations on violent revenge, psychiatric illness," social stressors and considerable planning before the offense. Previous to the offenses, murderers frequently communicate a final message to the media or the public (Knoll 8, 10, 14).

Questions

1. What is there about our society that encourages widespread exploitation of gun use?

2. Besides the predators, who are some of the main contributors to gun violence?

Facing obstacles to gun violence prevention

Embedded obstacles make violence extraordinarily hard to avert (Knoll 14, 17). Strict gun control is lacking. Legislatively, nothing has made a small difference until 2022 (Clyde and Miranda 2022). Highly coordinated actions by the National Rifle Association (NRA) and other national organizations are effective in preventing controls. And, more than 400 of our country's 3,080 sheriffs have signed a pledge to "oppose and disallow" new gun initiatives, as have sheriff associations in 15 states (Lenz 13).

1. How powerful are the obstacles? Explain.

2. What do you think is the effect of lobbying efforts?

Uvalde Violence

The largely Latino elementary school in Uvalde, Texas, cringed when the mass shooter killed 19 students and two teachers in 2022. When many law enforcement units waited for more than one hour to begin to capture the shooter, the country was "thrown into the abyss of sorrow, rage and despair" (Linfield SR3).

Social media, the press and even a former chief of Homeland Security offered this suggestion: "Photographs of the slaughtered children, whose faces and bodies were apparently mutilated beyond recognition, could be released to the public in hopes of garnering support for gun control legislation…The nation should be forced to see exactly what an AR-15 does to a child." Yet in perspective, it is essential to recall that "people, not photographs, create political change…Don't ask images to think, or to act, for you" (Linfield SR3).

Questions

1. What do you think added to the hesitancy of law enforcement? (Parents and friends cried out for a response.)

2. What might be the value of publicly depicting the bodies of mutilated, murdered children?

Community Efforts to Challenge Gun Violence Against Young People

Taking better initiatives to evaluate children from very young ages by experts can enhance clinical and educational decision-making. Improve the training of teachers, administrators, other school staff, pediatricians and parents about mental health issues. The coordination of school and mental health providers is also essential (Sandy 88).

As an each-day procedure, keep firearms out of the hands of youth. And cooperating groups and organizations need to inform gangs that if they carry guns, there will be efficient action by law enforcement (Carter 142-143).

A 2014 survey of the National Center for Education Statistics found that 88 percent of public schools had a written plan of how to respond to shooters, and 70 percent had drills to practice the plan. About 75 percent of our public schools use security cameras, and 43 percent employ weekly security personnel (Hefling 2). Some sheriffs and legislators have proposed harsh action against "Wild West" sheriffs who advocate refusing to enforce gun control laws (Lenz 17).

Remarkably, ten years after Australia legislated the removal of semiautomatic firearms, pump-action shotguns and rifles from civilians, there have been no mass shootings in their country (Knoll 17).

Exercise. School Violence – Sentence Completion

Talk about the responses to this exercise with several others. School gun-violence practices/policies could be positively addressed if

Students…

Administrators…

Teachers…

Parents…

School boards…

School social workers/school nurses…

Law enforcement…

Local government…

Physicians…

Priests/pastors/amans/rabbis…

Parent-teacher-organizations (PTO)…

Mass media…

Social media…

National Rifle Association (NRA)…

Coaches/janitors…

Student councils/student government boards…

Businesses...

Movie theaters...

Judges/lawyers/probation officers...

Now consider the essence of what may be behind a shooter's motivations and actions. Criminologists, Drs. James Densley and Julian Peterson, expertly provide their recent insights (Densley and Peterson 2022).

Densley articulated four steps in attempting to explain mass shooter's personal background.

1.	Early childhood trauma.

2.	Overlapping with later-life crises. Questioning their place in the world and having low self-esteem. Often suicidal or homicidal.

3.	Searching for persons who may make a big act quickly and/or final act. Identifying with an individual who performs mass shootings or observing a violent, radicalized manifesto online.

4.	Availability of firearms (Dickerson 2022).

Peterson suggested possible kinds of positive change interventions - crisis intervention training schools.

1.	Change the human relationships with school/other personnel.

2.	Work on a new mindset for those tempted toward violent actions.

Professor Rachael Snyder stipulates that a single priority for hope is "where all people can see the possibility of their own future...Broken things...can also be opportunities to rebuild," affirms Professor Snyder. Persons need to "have at least one person, just one adult, they can talk with (Snyder SR6).

Questions

1.	What do you think about Densley's analysis?

2.	What are your views about Peterson's intervention proposal?

3.	What do you think of Snyder's resolutions for hope?

Project - Humane Relationships in Sensitive and Potentially Explosive Gun Experiences

1. Why even get involved in potentially controversial settings?

2. What can you do to connect with lonely and/or distraught persons who might become dangerous persons and maybe report your concerns to appropriate authorities? **Be personally and vigilantly safe even with unexpected circumstances.**

3. How will you distinguish your engaged actions from being a rumor informant, intruder and an obtrusive monitor from being a balanced, concerned monitor and participant?

4. What can be your role as a potentially responsible citizen in addressing problematic situations?

5. Consider how you may or may not be making a difference in these violent gun-related circumstances?

New Gun Legislation

It took more than 30 years to achieve this new law on gun control. Limited in scope, it allows states to "petition courts to remove weapons from people deemed a threat to themselves or others...(It) prevents people convicted of domestic abuse from owning a gun...It expands background checks on people between the ages of 18 and 21 seeking to buy a gun (Clyde and Miranda 2022).

Questions

1. What checks on gun exploitation are missing in the 2022 law?

2. Explain why you think, or do not think, that a citizen's ability to access military rifles is considered appropriate?

Bullying

Question and comment

Next, ponder what you know about bullying. What are a few keywords that clarify what bulling means? Consider the interlocking framework of dominance and vulnerability. Discuss your feelings and thoughts with another person.

Definition

Bullying is an intentional act to repeatedly hurt and/or intimidate anyone perceived to be less powerful and vulnerable. Its frequency soars in transitional periods, especially between elementary and middle school (Gunter 1). One fifth of children and teens admit to being bullied or bulling, and it probably happens once in every seven minutes in a school environment (Shaw and Lee 504).

Among the needs bullying tries to meet are to control and have power. Bullying helps to determine one's place in a social hierarchy particularly in a new situation (Van 38). Why do kids bully? Sometimes they see themselves experiencing intimidations, threats to their power. Therefore, they see themselves as victims, that others are out-to-get them (Van 39).

Those bullied risk being more likely to have depression, behavioral disorders, substance abuse, and suicide. Sixty percent of boys who bully in middle school had at least one criminal conviction by age 24 (Van 39).

Exercise. Six Ways to Counter Bullying by Coordination with Others

Bullying can be more effectively countered by comprehensive, strategic initiatives. **First.** Bring parents into the process by providing educational "tool kits" and alerting them when it is known that their children are engaged in bullying (Holladay 44). **Second.** Use the best of the Seattle public school curriculum that confronts cyberbullying through a comprehensive preventive plan. It includes "debunking misconceptions, …building empathy, teaching safety skills and guiding young people in how to reject digital abuse. **Third.** Encourage students to apply the Golden Rule to develop creative mindsets that include abolishing binary thinking, e.g., "bullies are evil, victims are innocent." This can mean openly engaging youth about how aggressive actions are working for them and for others. Also, students can be educated on the long-term effects of bullying for educational and occupational success. **Fourth.** "Mentorship and buddy programs can help transitional students feel less fearful" (Van Del Valk 41). **Fifth.** Experiment with shifting from punitive to restorative approaches. The director of a school counseling program at the University of Arizona, Sheri Bauman, suggests using an international model called "Method of Shared Concern." It directly involves the bully, victim, bystanders, and trained staff (Holladay 44-45). **Sixth.** Expose students and teachers to videos like "Bullied," free to all schools through the Southern Poverty Law Center. It is the story of a bullied, yet persevering boy, who gains healing with justice. All this information applies to harassment with children of color.

Questions

1. Which of the six approaches seem most valid?

2. What do you think about the rationale behind the six ways to counter bullies?

3. Are there bullies or only persons who bully? What difference does it make when we distinguish persons who bully from labeling them as bullies? Explain.

Extremism - Context, Meaning and Impact of Recent Charlottesville Events

Raise no doubts that supremacy organizations are still very active, violent and cooperating with each other in 48 states. Recently, Charlottesville, Virginia, became the focal point of nationally publicized violence. Strategic to that dredged-up violence were far-right, extremist organizations. They can be identified as white nationalists, Neo-Nazis, Neo-Confederates and the Ku Klux Klan. All of them are currently active in Virginia (Staff 2022).

Many news organizations prefer using the term white nationalist rather than the Alt-Right. The amalgam of white nationalist factions, 'though diverse in some ways, shares a belief in separatism, white supremacy and proactive violence. This translates into espousing a Southern, white, segregated state/nation (Staff 6). And these supremacists are "obsessed with a purist form of identity...a white nation unpolluted by immigrant blood" (Polakowsuransky AR5).

Some consider that whites face extinction due to interracial marriage and non-white immigration. This belief is called white genocide, "an orchestrated eradication campaign" (Staff 6).

A new counterforce to Black Lives Matter is the white supremacist movement called White Lives Matter. Their slogan, "It's Not Racist to Live Your People," has been shared by groups like the Ku Klux Klan (KKK) (Viets 46). The violence of Neo-Nazis today invokes intense feelings for many, recalling holocaust victims and survivors. The original Nazi belief system identified the Aryan and the Jewish "races." Jews were considered non-human (Feagin 6).

Currently, they are anti-immigrant, anti-homosexual, racist and anti-Jewish. The Neo-Nazis "trace social problems to a Jewish conspiracy that supposedly controls governments, financial institutions and the media." Because of the deaths of leaders, and lawsuits by the SPLC, the numbers of the Neo-Nazis have been cut in half over the past 10 years (Potok and Williamson 46).

The Neo-Confederates originated in 1994. While the Neo-Confederates are only about 4% of all extremist groups, they also do not seem to grow (Potok and Williamson 53). Their platform has grown to be "distinctly racist, with the goal of building a theocratic South defined by the 'cultural dominance of the Anglo-Celtic (white) people and their institutions.'" Leaders advocate secession and oppose interracial marriage (Smith and Lenz 12, 14).

In addition, they have become more militant while encouraging families to stock up on assault weapons. Their leaders have stated, "Always act as if you are fighting in the last ditch for the survival of all you hold dear...We are already at war...," so states Michael Hill, a former history professor at an Alabama Black college. A weapons trainer of the Neo-Confederacy, John Weaver, reminds adherents that "God is the god of war...When God is involved, there is no failure" (Smith and Lenz, 12-13).

The Klan's repugnant history is filled with the historic swamp of extreme intimidation, rapes, lynchings and other murders, and the desolation of the African-American family. Jews, immigrants, homosexuals and Catholics are still under attack too. Remarkably, the number of KKK chapters has grown dramatically since 2014. Part of the reason is the denunciation of the Confederate battle flag and other Confederate symbols (Potok 41).

A counter organization to the supremacists is Antifa, derived from anti-Fascist. Their current leader, Mark Bray, states that their approach is "revolutionary self-defense." When attacked, they will use violent methods (Bray, Press, 2017). The anti-Fascist Antifa also argue that violence is occasionally justified when the "institutions of government fail to consistently halt Fascism" (Bray 169).

1. What may be the motivations of Supremacist and Antifa groups? Distinguish.

2. How do the methods of those opposing groups differ?

Charlottesville Conflict and Impact

The explosive drama in Charlottesville, Virginia, on August 11 and 12, 2017, began with the preparedness of white supremacists long before. On Friday, August 11, the consolidation of supremacist groups marched in Charlottesville in hooded garb, military green outfits, holding Confederate battle flags and banners exhibiting Nazi swastikas. Other banners read "Jews will not replace us," and "White is Right." Some carried assault weapons (Dowd SR11).

In the fearful darkness of that Charlottesville night, at least a few hundred torch-carrying supremacists surrounded students holding a large banner saying, "VA Students Against White Supremacy." Also, the supremacists clashed with counter-protestors over the issue of removing the statue of Confederacy General Robert E. Lee on the campus. Other goals of the supremacists were to draw media attention, intimidate, and bond (Morris A1).

The Saturday morning encounters began peacefully. "Religious leaders, Black Lives Matter activists and other groups chanted, sang songs and carried their own signs." Yet, violence erupted when phalanges of supremacists brandishing shields and wearing helmets kept charging counter-protestors in Charlottesville's Emancipation Park. The local police could not control the brawl. The sheriff's department, state police and the Virginia National Guard were recruited. And the City of Charlottesville declared a state of emergency (Stolberg and Rosenthal 1).

As the rally was dispersing, a car allegedly driven by white supremacist James Alex Field, Jr. rammed into counter-protestors, injuring 19 and killing Heather Heyer. "After that it was pandemonium" (Stolberg and Rosenthal 1).

1. Was there any likelihood to preventing the Charlottesville violence. Explain.

2. What do you think was the initial plan of the Nationalists?

Responses

The responses to Charlottesville's experiences were profoundly different. Former President Trump said that there was "hatred, bigotry and violence on many sides." National politicians, and others, challenged Trump's response for suggesting that the violent intentions and actions were seemingly equal. And he did not otherwise specifically criticize the White Nationalists by name as those who were responsible for the rally (Stack A15), (Stolberg and Rosenthal 14), (Thrush and Haberman 14).

Key relatives of Robert E. Lee, Jefferson Davis and Stonewall Jackson asserted that the statues can go. None agreed with Trump, and other Americans argued that removing the statues "would be an affront to history and heritage." Two great-great-grandsons of Jackson said, "We are ashamed to benefit from white supremacy while our Black family and friends suffer..." They called Confederate statues "overt symbols of racism and white supremacy" (Astor and Fandos 14).

A Black museum curator framed her response as a scholar. "There are people who see them as symbols of virtue. They are persons who made sacrifices for them." Kristy Colemen, the CEO of The American Civil War Museum in Richmond, Virginia, also said, "We dance with what is. History is always a process of new questions. As scholars, we try to go back to the historical record and the questions left us, and try to answer them. It would be irresponsible if we did not go back and see what we now understand as things in a bigger picture" (Melber 2017).

Kristin Szakos, a white Charlottesville City Council member said, "The statues are symbols to perpetuate slavery. That's what they are celebrated for. The statues are in full regalia against the United States" (Melber 2017).

Even the 2017 Miss America Pageant included two questions relevant to Charlottesville. Judges queried contestants about Civil War statues and the responses by Donald Trump to the Charlottesville violence (NBC 2017).

The Episcopalian National Cathedral in Washington, D.C. has decided to remove two, stained-glass windows depicting Robert E. Lee and Stonewall Jackson within the sanctuary. Studying the place of Confederate symbols for one year, the Charlottesville experience hastened a sense of urgency about the Church's decision (Cochran A15).

Questions

1. Why do you think there has been such a broad impact to the actions at Charlottesville?

2. How do the consciences of some groups make a difference in the changes by those groups?

White Supremacists on College Campuses

Ponder what it takes for administrators and faculty across the country to strategically grapple with a full-blown spike in white supremacy on campuses. Vanguard America is a leading white supremacist recruiter in colleges and universities (ADL 2017).

"Dozens of college presidents have sent letters to incoming students to reiterate their commitment to tolerance." And the recent racist violence at Charlottesville has forced higher education to more urgently reckon with "competing values: safety, free speech and a commitment to tolerance and diversity" (Baumgaertner 17).

Jonathan Greenblatt, CEO of the Anti-Defamation League, stated his organization "cataloged 115 incidents of white supremacist propaganda on American campuses between January and April, 2017, up from nine during the same four months in 2016...They openly boast about efforts to create a physical presence on campuses where students are engaged in the war of ideas" (Baumgaertner 17).

1. What do you believe that white supremacists can achieved with propaganda on campuses?

2. What other methods may they use?

Historically, Congress voted unanimously to condemn white supremacist organizations and their violent action in Charlottesville about a month after the upheaval. Donald Trump did sign the "nonbinding Congressional Resolution urging him to condemn groups like white supremacists and the KKK. Yet, earlier in the day, he said that "those who resisted Neo-Nazis and white supremacists were as much to blame as opposing crowds" (Landler 1).

1. What actions may be taken to confront the supremacists (Benjamin 2017)?

2. How do you account for Donald Trump's stating that the opposing groups should be treated equally and the blame for actions should be shared?

Naomi Klein, author and activist, and others have asserted that there is strength in numbers. Others have suggested that there needs to be at least 500 persons to counter supremacists. Klein also reflects that the most targeted communities should not "be the only ones standing up to these forces" (Abramsky 17).

Bree Newsome, the black woman who removed a Confederate flag from the flagpole at the South Carolina statehouse, thinks more allies should be protesting. She said that "white people were putting themselves on the front lines Charlottesville." When white people protest, they are more likely to attract media attention (Cox 58). And legendary photographer, Lee Friedlander, showed how monuments hide in plain sight: subsumed by traffic, by familiarity…" (Dyer 16).

Reflections/Questions

1. What are lessons to be learned from the Charlottesville experience?

2. What do you think may be the impact of "standing up for others?"

3. What do you think are some implications of Donald Trump's signing the Congressional Resolution and yet stating contradictory views to the Congressional leaders about the responsibility for Charlottesville violence?

4. What should be the extent of freedom of expression when harm is intended? Think about Charlottesville, and speeches on college campuses by white supremacists that are cases in point.

Concluding Overview

"Violence is collectively enabled, has a collective impact, and requires a collective response" (Mingus 19). The Reverend Richard Barber says that he "believes that cross-racial, cross-religious, and cross-general coalitions are the only way to confront…violence…For him, all forms of oppression overlap" (Blow 10). The reality of the dangerous prevalence and patterns of violence in society can be disheartening and overwhelming. Yet, we may acknowledge the vitality and commitment of those who will not let violence have the final word.

Reader's Wrap Up, Story, and Questions

As you continue to tell your story, what feelings and thoughts are prominent? Do you find changes in your approaches to violence and nonviolence? Explain. How do you think the content and procedures of this chapter touch upon your daily experiences?

Project

Construct a practical project which specifically focuses on possible violence in the reader's local setting. Be sure to include how violence can be constructively addressed. Consulting with others in the development of the project can be valuable.

Works Cited

Abramsky, Sasha. "When Violence Comes." THE NATION, 23 Oct. 2017, p. 17.

Adetiba, Elizabeth. "Q&A Tarana Burke." THE NATION. Apr/Nov. 2017, p. 5.

ADL. "White Supremacists on Campus: Unprecedented Recruitment Efforts Underway." 9 Jun. 2017.

Astor, Maggie and Nicholas Fandos. "Descendants Say Confederate Statues Can Go." NYT, 20 Aug. 2017, p.14

Baumgaertner, Emily. "Colleges Ponder Action After Virginia." NYT, 10 Sep. 2017, p.17.

Benjamin, Rich. "The Beat." MSNBC, 13 Sep. 2017.

Blair, Garet, Anya Zoledziowski and the News21 Staff. "Murdered and Missing: Note American Indian Women Challenge the police and Courts." CENTER FOR POLICE INTEGRITY, 27 Aug. 2018.

Blow, Charles M. "Walking with a Modern Day Moses." NYT, 13 Mar. 2022, p. SR10.

Bouie, Jemelle. "It Took a Century to Get an Anti-Lynching Bill." NYT, 3 Apr. 2022, p. SR9.

Bray, Mark. ANTIFA: ANTI-FASCIST HANDBOOK." Melville House, 2017, p. 169.

—, "Meet the Press Daily." MSNBC, 26 Aug. 2017.

Carter, Greg Lee. "Boyhood in America." in Kathleen Tiemann et al (editors). THE INTERSECTION COLLECTION. Pearson Custom Publishing, 2011, pp. 135-140.

Chozich, Amy. "Dunham-Clinton Rift Revealed." NYT, 10 Dec. 2017, p. ST1.

Clyde, Don and Shauneen Miranda. "Biden Signs Gun Safety Bill into Law." NPR, 22 June 2022.

Coates, Ta Nehisi. BETWEEN THE WORLD AND ME. Spiegel and Grau, 2015, p. 7.

Cochran, Emily. "National Cathedral Will Remove Windows That Honor Confederate Generals." NYT, 7 Sept. 2017, p. A15.

Cox, Ana Marie. "Bree Newsome Thinks Allies Should Be Protesting." NYT Magazine, 22 Oct. 2017, p. 58.

"Crisis on Campus," Dateline NBC TV, 20 Jun. 2015.

Densley, James and Julian Peterson. CBS, Sunday Morning Show, 12 Jun. 2022.

DeVeaux, Thomson Amelia. "The Lonely Quest of Mary Koss." THE NATIONAL JOURNAL MAGAZINE. Washington, D. C., 2 May. 2015, p. 4.

Dowd, Maureen. "Trump, Neo-Nazis and the Klan." NYT, 20 Aug. 2017, p. SR11.

Dyer, Geoff. "Long Before America's Monuments Became Central to a National Debate, Lee Friedlander Reminded Us that They Were Hiding in Plain Sight." NYT Magazine, 15 Oct. 2017, p.16.

Editors. "Between the World and Me." Book Cover, 2015.

Elving, Ron. "The U.S. Once had a Ban on Assault Weapons - Why Did It Expire?" NPR, 13 Aug. 2019.

Erikson, Eric. GANDHI'S TRUTH. W. W. Norton and Company, 1969, pp. 196-198, 225, 237.

Fischer, Louis. THE ESSENTIAL GANDHI. Vintage Books, 1962, p. 87.

Fulton, Sybrina and Tracy Martin. REST IN POWER. Random House, 2017.

Gandhi, Mohandas K. AN AUTOBIOGRAPHY. Beacon Press, 1959, p. 407, 504-505.

Grose, Charles. Interview with David Hogg in Minneapolis. 2020.

Gunter, Booth. "Suit Arises to Stop Bullying in Mississippi School." SPLC REPORT, Spring, 2014, Vol 44, No 1, p. 1.

Hefling, Kimberly. "Schools Increase the Use of Safety Drills, Security." STAR TRIBUNE, 22 May 2015, p. 2.

Hess, Amanda. "Defying the 'Open Secret.'" NYT, 3 Dec. 2017, p. AR1, p. 18.

Holladay, Jennifer. "Bullying." TEACHING TOLERANCE, Fall, 2010, Issue 38, p. 43.

Katz, J. I AM THE FIRE OF TIME: THE VOICES OF NATIVE AMERICAN WOMEN. P. Dutton, 1977, p. 6.

King Center, The. 2015.

Kizzire, Jamie. "Guide Helps Bystanders Counter Hate Incidents." SPLC, Winter, 2017, p. 5.

Knefel, Molly. "Incarceration Vs. Education." THE NATION, 11 May. 2015, pp. 22, 24.

Knoll, James IV. "Mass Murder," in Charles Scott (editor). FORSENIC PSYCHIATRY. University of Michigan Press, 2012, pp. 8, 10, 14.

Kochman, Thomas. BLACK AND WHITE CONFLICT STYLES. University of Chicago Press, 1981, p. 58.

Landler, Mark. "Trump Resurrects His Claim That Both Sides Share Blame in Charlottesville Violence." NYT, 15 Sep. 2017, p.1.

Lenz, Ryan. "Battle Lines. SPLC, Summer, 2013, p. 14.

Linfield, Susie. "Show Us the Victims of Uvalde." NYT, 5 Ju. 2022, p. SR3.

Liptak, Allan. "Who Will Judge?" NYT, 12 Apr. 2015, p. 6.

Little, Anita. "Passing the Test." MS MAGAZINE, 2015, p. 11.

McCollum, Sean. "Country Outposts." TEACHING TOLERANCE, Fall, 2010, Issue 38, p. 33.

Melber, Ira. Interview by Joy Reeve. MSNBC, 17 Aug. 2017.

Mingus, Mia. "Transformative Justice." FELLOWSHIP, Vol. 78, No. 2, Winter, 2021-2022, p. 19

Morris, Wesley. "In Virginia and on TV, A Supremacist Summer." NYT, 27 Aug. 2017, p. AR1.

MTV Daily, MSNBC, 8 Apr. 2022.

NBC, "Miss America Pageant." 10 Sep. 2017.

Newman, David. SOCIOLOGY. Pine Forge Press, 2008.

O'Hare, Callaghan. "Mental Illness Is Not Useful Means Predict Gun Violence." NYT, 22 Aug. 2022, p. 7.

Patterson, Orlando. "The Real Problem with America's Inner Cities." NYT, 10 May. 2015, p. SR6.

Polakowsuransky, Sasha. "White Nationalism Is the Real Threat to the West - Not Jihad." NYT, 15 Oct. 2017, p. AR5.

Potok, Mark and Alex Williamson. "The Year in Hate and Extremism." SPLC, Intelligence Report, Spring, 2016, pp. 41, 53.

Proclamation No. 8769,77, Federal Regulation 211, 28 Dec. 2011.

Reeve, Joy. Interview with Christopher Cantwell. NBC News, 15 Aug. 2017.

Roberson, Campbell. "A Lynching Memorial Is Opening. The Country has Never Seen Anything Like It." NYT, 25 Apr. 2018, p. 27.

Rosenberg, Russell. NONVIOLENT COMMUNICATION. Puddle Dancer Press, 1999, pp. 1, 225-226.

"Shooting at Sandy Hook Elementary School." Report of the Connecticut Office of Child Advocacy, 21 Nov. 2014, p. 88.

Sicha, Choire. "Going Down in Infamy." NYT BOOK REVIEW, 19 Apr. 2015, p. 13.

Smith, Janet and Ryan Lenz. "New Soldiers of the New Confederacy." SPLC, Intelligence Report, Winter, 2011, pp. 12, 14.

Staff, "Alt-Right." SPLC, Intelligence Project, Sep. 2016, p. 6.

Stolberg, Sheryl Day and Brian M. Rosenthal. "White Nationalist Protest Leads to Deadly Violence." NYT, 13 Aug. 2017, p. 1.

Thrush, Glenn and Maggie Haberman. "Critics Slam Trump's Tepid Condemnation of "Violence on 'Many sides' in Virginia." NYT, 13 Aug. 2017, p. 14.

"Today at the Trade Deadline: Let the Sellers Beware As Well." STAR TRIBUNE, 30 July. 2014, p. C2.

Tougas, Joe. "Finding a Home and History." TODAY, Spring 2022, p. 219.

Van Der Valk, Adrienne. "There Are No Bullies." TEACHING TOLERANCE, Fall, 2013, Issue 45, p. 38.

Viets, Sarah. "White Lives Matter," SPLC, Intelligence Report, Summer, 2016, p. 46.

Westerman, Gwen. MINI SOTA MAKOCE: THE DAKOTA IN MINNESOTA, Minnesota History Society Press, 2018.

—, "Letter from the Director." NALS, Minnesota, Prior Lake, 2 Mar. 2017.

WH.Gov 2022.

Yang, Jeff. "When Victims and Suspects Are Asian American." NYT, 29 Jan. 2023, p. SR7.

Chapter 6

Early Social Change Movements

How consequential are the unknown, hidden parts of our racial movements? This chapter brings many unknown racial experiences to light.

Defining social change and social movements

Social change is a transformative experience of culture and institutions over time (Macionis 436). A social movement is a "continuous, large-scale, organized collective action motivated by the desire to enact, to stop, or to reverse social change in everyday life" (Newman 467).

Reflection. Exercise.

Compare/contrast social change and social movements. This means pondering critically, and writing the essential similarities and differences between the definitions of social change and social movements.

Eric Hoffer, labor activist of many years past, posits those superior individuals, and outcasts at the other extreme, shape major changes in a country. The misfits and minorities do not change themselves. Rather, they try to change the world. He states that "we shall go on believing that man, unlike other forms of life, is not a captive of his past...but is possessed of infinite plasticity, and his potentialities for good and for evil are never wholly exhausted" (Hoffer 101, 120).

Comment on Hoffer's views of change by the disadvantaged, and his views of the past and the future.

Women's Suffrage Movement

Suffrage Granted in 1920

Travel with me to New Zealand where the pioneer of women's suffrage in the Western World occurred in 1893. Maori (Polynesian) and Pakeha (white) residents equally were granted the right to vote. When I toured New Zealand, I saw the bas relief statue of several women taking a barrel of petitions to promote the right to vote to the government. Kate Sheppard led the group of international advocates (Grose 2011).

"The Women's Movement is the premier liberation movement of modern times, an appeal for social transformation which will radically reshape society," declared Walter Rauschenbucsh and Shailer Mathews in the late 1800s. That was the right to vote in the U.S. (Lindsey 207-208).

Among the white leaders was Frances Willard, long-term president of the Women's Christian Temperance Union (W.C.T.U.). She rallied the support of the W.C.T.U. for women's right to vote as an instrument to heal the wounds of the country (Evans 46).

Even a few white men supported the women's right to vote in the late 1800s. And reasons for full women's rights emerged from leaders of the Christian Social Gospel Movement. Those leaders, Rauschenbusch and Mathews, declared that "women must become political agents...Those leaders assumed that the entry of women would make politics more clean...and humane" (Lindsey 208).

When rights are granted to all, and laws are applied universally, then freedom and suffrage offer "needed restraint on greed and the lust for power..." of white men. Theologian Reinhold Niebuhr affirmed, "Man's capacity for justice makes democracy possible but man's inclination to injustice makes democracy necessary" (Spann 21).

Questions

1. What do you think about Hoffer's view that misfits and minorities do not change themselves? Rather, they try to change the world.

2. Comment on Niebuhr's quote about justice, injustice, and democracy.

An Alternative Black Women's Movement Cannot be Hidden

In context, "white women's views about voting were seen as a symbol of essential purity with their husbands and brothers. Black women were seeking the ballot for themselves and their men as a means of empowering the Black community" (Staples SR4).

The stunning and predictable exclusion of African Americans from the white women's suffrage movement is infrequently recorded. Elizabeth Cady Stanton and Susan B. Anthony's racist views, among those of other white women leaders, were evident in white movement activities.

White women leaders of the 1913 Washington, D. C. parade demanded that Black marchers all be gathered in the back of the parade. Black leader Ida B. Wells refused to participate, while many other Blacks did. And Mary Ann Cary, a Black feminist, wrote to the white, National Women's Suffrage Association requesting that the names of 94 Black women be signors of the Women's Declaration of Sentiments. That document demanded the immediate enfranchisement of all American women. Yet, the names of all the African American women were not included (Staples SR4).

As a result, Black women organized their own local clubs for suffragist action. The clubs showed their strength in demonstrations that included several thousand members overall (Staples SR4). If Black clubs associated with the white movement, white women thought it might anger Southerners (Staples SR4).

Questions

1. What was in the white suffragist's background which contributed to their discriminatory views and actions?

2. How well-known has been the information on Black suffragists? Comment.

Mary Ann Cary, the Black journalist and activist, sent a blunt letter to famous African American advocate Frederick Douglass at the time of Elizabeth Cady Stanton's 1848 strategic conference and the Declaration of Sentiments. "We should do more and talk less," affirmed Cary. She wrote that Blacks should stop whining about our afflictions. For so long almost nothing has improved about our suffrage rights. African Americans were often marginalized as a powerful force. And that same year, Cary led a group of Black women to the Congressional Judiciary Committee petitioning the right to vote (Specia obit).

Questions

1. Why do you think that Cary and others considered that their efforts could make a difference?

2. Frederick Douglas cut to the quick the fallacy of the white suffrage viewpoint; being that "African American women could magically separate their blackness from their femaleness" (Specia obit). What do you think he meant by this?

Another Black leader, Dr. W.E.B. DuBois, clarified the differences between white women suffragists and the Black men and women. White suffragist women took a hand's off approach to Black suffragists. "Do not touch the Negro problem. That will offend the South. Those white suffragists desired to increase unity for their cause. And they wanted to the issue of women suffragists and Black suffragist separate" (Watkins 16).

DuBois further stipulated that Blacks should fully support white women suffragists. He reasoned that votes for white women meant the vote for Black women. "Every argument for Negro suffragists is an argument for women suffragists. We are facing the great question of right in which personal hatreds have no place" (Watkins 19). Such was his inter-connected and compassionate thinking.

1. According to DuBois, what was the central difference between the views of white women suffragists and the ideas of Black women suffragists?

2. What do you think about DuBois' logic and caring about women's suffrage? Explain.

Voting Project

Participate with a voter organization in your community. If you are in a large city, the community office in a Chinatown or an American Indian center can identify ways you may engage with their voting program. Latinos and Blacks also have local community centers or associations.

Interview a staff member or a few volunteers about voting in a local organizational center, political or non-political. Briefly journal.

Or you could accompany a voting canvasser who goes to houses preferably in a people-of-color neighborhood. Also, the League of Women Voters is a non-partisan organizational contact.

Eugenics Movement

Is it possible that Eugenics laws remain in 13 states by 2023? Francis Galton originated the idea of eugenics in 1883 in England. It grew under U.S. Dr. Henry Goddard and other physicians. Eugenics is "defined as an applied science that is directed toward the genetic potential improvement of the human species" (Cashmore 125). "White elites believed that American life would be improved by increased inbreeding of Anglo Saxons and Nordics whom they assumed had high IQs." If persons did not fit into this standard of racial perfection, they became targets of eugenics programs. In the late 1800s, those considered "unfit included Blacks, Indigenous people, poor whites, most immigrants, and people with disabilities (Stern 2020).

In the early 1900s, men with disabilities, poor men, and men of color were the main focus of eugenicists (Kaebler 2). In most of the 50 states, federally supported eugenic boards even promoted sterilization during the 1900s (Mahjeshwar 2). Even teaching hospitals recruited medical students to perform sterilizations. They became perversions of medical practice.

Noteworthy, sterilization also was practiced in prisons and institutional homes for the disabled (Manjsehwar 1).

In the mid-1900s when information about reproductive rights was outlawed, Margaret Sanger was rejected by women's rights groups. This was during the Suffrage Movement. She broadened her alliances with eugenics groups to make the use of contraceptives respectable and widespread. She even aligned herself with the racial and hierarchical beliefs of the Eugenics Movement (Alonso 2).

Nazi Germany too was informed by U.S. sterilization laws. A stepping stone to the Holocaust was compulsory sterilization of about 400,000 women and children, mostly Jews, between 1934 and 1945 in Germany (Kaebler 1); (Stern 2020).

A counter-eugenics movement in the 1940s culminated in the Supreme Court's decision that "rejected eugenic sterilization as a valid state goal and recognized that procreation is a basic civil right. Yet, the law in the Supreme Court's Bell decision still remains on the books (News ADA 2022).

Hospitals were segregated by race until the 1950s. Desegregation resulted in a backlash from white supremacists for racial control and racial hierarchies. This meant potential control of Black reproduction by sterilization (Stern 2020).

By the 1960s, women were about 99% of sterilization cases. Black women, the poor and disabled surged in number at that time. It is estimated that 25-50% of Black women were sterilized between 1970 and 1976 (Kaebler 2).

During the Twentieth Century more than 60,000 persons were sterilized in 32 states" (Stern 2020). For example, in 2020, more than 40 Latina women initiated written statements of their invasive medical procedures without their approval under Immigration and Customs Enforcement (I.C.E.) (Immigration Review 2021).

A medical student at the Los Angeles County/USC Medical Center witnessed and testified about what she viewed as the Medical Center's concerted effort to reduce the birth rate of racial minorities. The doctor would hold a syringe in front of a woman in labor and under the throes of contractions...ask if she wanted a painkiller. He would say, "Do you want to have to go through this pain again? Sign the papers." Problematically, these consent forms were administered in English to Mexican American women. In a lawsuit, women alleged that medical personnel systematically coerced Mexican American women into submitting to sterilization (News ACLU 1-2).

The allegation of coerced sterilization in I.C.E. detention facilities is a form of injustice inflicted upon immigration detainees as late as the 1990s (News ACLU).

Questions

1. Why did some doctors, some social workers, and all levels of government agree to implementing the ideology of sterilization?

2. Why did not vulnerable persons rise up to challenge sterilization?

3. Why has the history of sterilization largely been unknown?

4. What makes change so slow in addressing sterilization?

5. Why was the ethical issue of "without consent" not commonly addressed?

6. How would you explore whether sterilization is practiced today? Research this issue.

Sharecropper Fannie Lou Hamer's response after sterilization further motivated her activism. Hamer was sterilized, without consent, while under anesthesia in the hospital at age 27 (Manjeshwar 2). Subsequently, she dynamically lifted her life into a life-long career of civil rights and political activism.

While in her voting rights activism, she was brutally attacked. That damaged her eyes, legs and liver until her death (Manjeshwar 1).

Charlie Cobb of the Student Non-Violent Coordinating Committee (SNCC) created and helped develop 30 Freedom Schools that began in Mississippi in the summer of 1964. Fannie Lou Hamer, and the parents of those schools, soon took on the idea of the Freedom Democratic Party (FDP) (Zinn 247).

They claimed that those seats traditionally held by white Mississippians kept Negroes out of the Party machinery. Therefore, their proposal to the Democratic Party's Credentials Committee was to seat representatives of the FDP rather than the regular Mississippi delegation (Zinn 251-252).

Political gyrations whirled uniquely at the 1964 Democratic Convention at Atlantic City due in part to the actions of the FDP. The Credentials Committee took on extreme pressure from the new President L. B. Johnson regarding the official seating of FDP members at the Convention. The President deemed the FDP's request politically questionable partly because of his expected pressure from Southern party members (Branch PILLAR, 473).

A compromise was proposed which only would allow representation from two members at large of the FDP. Later, FDP members slipped through security and took over the Mississippi delegation seats. They were ousted from their short-term sit-in, and demonstrations occurred outside. The final vote of the delegates rejected the proposal of the FDP. Leader Hamer declared, "We didn't come all this way for no two seats" (Branch PILLAR, 475).

There was a new kind of politics for the FDP by 1965, called protest politics. It "exerted its force both against and within the traditional politics" (Zinn 261).

How striking is it that Hamer's sterilization helped motivate her longstanding hope, and powerful activism.

Questions

1. What do you think motivated Hamer to become a political activist?
2. What was the role of the Black community in developing the FDP?
3. Why do you believe the FDP invested so much to attempt the radical change in the Democratic Party?

Residential Schools for Children in First Nation (Canada) and (U.S.) American Indian Communities

The Canadian government's assimilation process meant that at least 150,000 First Nation children were forcefully taken from their indigenous families and restricted to only living in government-funded, Catholic-administered "residential schools" (Change 2022). And at least 4,000 Indigenous children were forced to die. This occurred between the mid-1800s and the late 1900s (Change 2022).

The children said that "you had a lot of mental challenges...because you grew up without your community, ...without the power of your people, and the strength of your language, your ceremonies, and your traditions," according to the head of the National Center for Truth and Reconciliation, Stephanie Scott (Change 2022).

After numerous requests from indigenous organizations and leaders, Pope Francis came to indigenous Canadian lands to apologize to First Nation survivors and leaders. What the Pope said, among other points, was "I have come to your native land to tell you in person of my sorrow, to implore God's forgiveness, healing and reconciliation" (Change 2022). And Francis declared, "This disastrous error was incompatible with the Gospel of Jesus Christ" (Winfield and Smith 2022). Pope Francis also articulated that the Catholic

Church cannot demand the "European way of expressing faith" (Winfield and Smith 2022).

Others have stated that the Pope did not say enough. They wanted him to say that" they (Vatican) were going to make reparations, …return land, and…needs to have actions." Some indigenous people declared there should be actions by the Vatican (Change 2022).

The Canadian government paid reparations of billions of dollars that meant transferring lands to First Nation peoples. And the Canadian Catholic dioceses and religious orders provided $50 million and plan for many million more (Winfield and Smith 2022).

Many Catholic theologians disagree about the responsibility of the whole Church. Is it accountable for the negative acts of all Catholics or are only accountable local members? Consider the idea that the body of Christ, the Church, is itself, sinless. This could mean that the Pope was saying that "he was asking forgiveness for the actions of members of the Church but not the institution in its entirety," according to Canadian scholar Jeremy Bergen (Winfield and Smith 2022). Similarly, should the Vatican provide reparations and other forms of responsibility or leave those duties to local dioceses and orders?

First Nation leaders declared that the legacy of abuse was the root cause of alcohol and drug addiction (Winfield and Smith 2022). Think of the heavy emotional toll experienced by the children, their families, and First Nation communities.

Questions

1. What do you think was lacking from Pope Francis' speech and actions in Canada?

2. In what ways was Pope Francis' visit of value to the Canadian First Nation people?

3. What do you think may been the consequences of the "residential schools" on future First Nation life? Why may there have been a cause-and-effect relationship?

4. How do you think that the Catholic Church, and its members, could justify their beliefs with their actions concerning "residential schools" at those times? Explain and journal.

In the U.S., the 804 "boarding schools" were traumatizing and violent similar to those of Canada. That action was widespread in the U.S. and included the government and Christian organizations. Extending westward, those children's schools included Alaska Natives and Native Hawaiians (Haagland 2021).

As a result, the children's culture was erased through the process of forced assimilation (Haagland 2021). Overall, the approach was described as militarizing and used identity-alteration methods. Punishment included solitary confinement, whipping, cuffing, limits on food, sexual abuse and sterilization (Manjeshwar 3; Newland 12, 92-95). The indigenous children survived in those inter-generational internment facilities from the mid-1800s through the late 1900s (Interior 2022).

U.S. Secretary of Interior, Deb Haaland, instructed the Interior Department in 2022 to begin researching the lives of boarding-school survivors. This widespread action will include survivors "stories, connecting communities with trauma-oriented support, and facilitating a permanent collection of oral history" (Interior 2022). It was 1978 when those schools of abuse closed, and children could reunite with their families (Schaefer 162).

Questions

1. What are a few key differences between the information about Canadian and U.S. indigenous children?

2. What factors may have contributed to more than a century of the federal government's decisions to begin and continue indigenous "boarding schools"?

3. Why was there not more opposition to "boarding schools" and "residential schools" by the indigenous peoples?

Busses Became Fully Accessible for Blacks as Well as Whites - Rosa Parks

Can you imagine that four Black women and the 15-year-old, Claudette Colvin, had refused to give up their seats for white passengers nine months before the dramatic actions of Rosa Parks. Ann Robinson, an English professor at Alabama State University, Montgomery, was instrumental in the release of Colvin from jail (King 42).

Beyond the Supreme Court's Brown V. Board of Education declaration that school segregation was unconstitutional in 1954, Parks was deeply affected by the brutal death of Emmett Till in 1955 (Parks REFUSE, 232, 236, 240). After Till apparently whistled at a white woman, three white men "cracked the whip, pulled the trigger, washed blood from the truck, threw away his shoes that would not burn, tied a fan around his neck, and cast his body into the Tallahatchie River" (Wilks 3).

The men were acquitted, but the story gained nation coverage in the early days of TV and LOOK Magazine. Till's mother allowed pictures of his body in the casket to be visibly shown to the world. (Bellamy 2, "Eyes" 19). Carolyn Bryant, the young man's accuser, confessed more than 60 years later that her "claims were false." She also confessed that "nothing that boy did could ever justify what happened to him" (Perez-Pena A13).

What made Park's action different was for the first time the bus driver called the police. She could have followed the driver's typical determination to stand up in the back of the bus or get off the bus. Whites "sat from the forward toward the rear; blacks sat from the back forward." This occasion she would have had to stand over the seat she had just vacated. She just refused "to obey the driver when he said, 'Stand up'" (Parks, REFUSE, 230-233). She went to jail and was later released.

The even more complicated events following Park's action will be greatly condensed. A small group of Blacks met and called for a boycott. On Saturday, 200 volunteers distributed leaflets door-to-door in the Black community. Robinson covered the two Black high schools. A Black-domestic servant shared a leaflet with her white employer. Then, the white employer submitted the "information to the MONTGOMERY ADVERTISER newspaper, and the story hit the Sunday front-page paper" (Clark, REFUSE 232, 240).

On the early busses, there were no passengers in the Black areas. This was the initial "time in Montgomery history that Blacks acted together to resist racial injustice" (Abernathy 146).

For the comprehensively engaged Black community, a few new changes in training and scheduling were all engrossing. Sessions in non-violence were led by King, and young leader James Lawson, two times a week in churches for about a year. Gospel music, spirituals and the Black national anthem (Lift Every Voice and Sing…) added zest and inspiration to each event (King 216, 84-49).

Imagine how the Black parents' personal lives were turned upside down. Less sleep, children's schedules, new complexity and confusion, added physical pain, more financial responsibility, and more time away from home were among the changes. It took 381 boycotting days to bring resolution. On November 13, 1956, the U.S. Supreme Court declared that Alabama's state and local segregated bussing laws were unconstitutional (King 160, 164).

James Farmer said that "King's Montgomery protest not only repudiated the violent machismo of America, it also stirred to awaken another America - the America of Emerson, of Thoreau, of Quakers, of the abolitionists, and the America of principle and compassion" (Farmer 186). A reviewer of a book about Parks asked us to remember Rosa Parks as one who "believed in collective action over individual celebrity" (Donham 81). The action of Rosa Parks lifted social change beyond imagination, according to Dr. King (King 69).

Reflection. Exercise.

Those who boycotted buses in Montgomery for over one year were able to consistently remain peaceful because (add to the word/phrases below.)

Black churches...

Black ministers...

Black leaders...

Black followers...

Alabama State A&T College...

city bus line...

Montgomery government representatives...

some local whites (especially women)...

media...

and...

Reflect on and discuss with others on several ways in which the Montgomery experience was monumental for the Civil Rights Movement and the U.S.,

Questions

1. What made the death of Emmett Till so strategic to Parks and bus desegregation?

2. Although others preceded Parks in going against segregated seating on local buses, what made her actions an instrumental part of the Civil Rights Movement?

3. What was behind the capability of grassroots Blacks to take on being marchers?

4. Why has Rosa Parks presently become such a notable symbol in U.S. public lore?

5. What made the role of James Lawson so crucial to the success of the bus desegregation tactics?

Freedom Riders and Inter-State Buses

James Farmer led many civil rights initiatives with his group known as The Congress of Racial Equality (C.O.R.E.) A few hundred volunteers were recruited and trained in non-violent action for C.O.R.E.'s Freedom Rider's project (Farmer 1-32). One of the Black, potential riders conversed with me about the uncertainty and sacrifice of being a rider. (I had a family of three young boys and decided not to join the Freedom Riders movement because my family was my priority). (Grose, Yale student 1961).

A Black theological student, John Lewis was one of many Freedom Riders who rode on Trailways buses to desegregate inter-state buses in 1961. Leaving Washington, D. C., their first stop was in South Carolina. There, Lewis was the first rider to be attacked. Hit, bruised and kicked, Lewis ended on the pavement while bleeding from his head. Others were similarly hurt during this violent journey across the South (Farmer 197).

> The following illustration of empathy is a symbol of hope and a call to action. The musical, "The Parchman Hour," tells the story of the Freedom Riders in Mississippi who sacrificed life and limb for equality on interstate buses. Many were college students, black and white, who were arrested and then also brutalized and humiliated while confined in Parchman Penitentiary. During their weeks of incarceration, they sang freedom songs daily and held hunger strikes when they had already lost much of their physical strength. Professor Lucas declares in this musical Program, "We cannot merely marvel at what those in the Civil Rights Movement did for us; we must root out the injustices which surround us today… If we admire the Freedom Riders, then we must seek to become them in new ways and unexpected places" (Lucas 13).

So, empathy, as framed within the "Parchman Hour" drama, can lead to empathic action.

Questions

1. Would you have considered being a volunteer during the Freedom Riders' experiences? Explain.

2. How may engaging injustice be empathy in action?

3. What do you think inspired those inmates in the Mississippi Parchman Penitentiary?

John Lewis' leadership included consequential actions with local and national support, and collective cooperation. Among those selected for the Gandhian Award for non-violence were a member of the core leadership team for the "March on Washington for Jobs and Freedom," the president of the Student Non-violent Coordinating Committee (student lunch-counter sit-ins), the leader of the Selma to Montgomery march for voting rights, a congressional representative from Atlanta, Georgia, and many more. Many of Lewis' ways were to pitch and stir up actions for everyone's universal rights. Part of an astute quote of his ended by declaring, "Make trouble, make good trouble, make necessary trouble, and redeem the souls of America (Wesley Lewis ABA 2021).

President John Kennedy confirmed an Order of the Interstate Commerce Commission that enforced inter-state rights to travel for "colored" and "whites" on November 1, 1961 (Farmer 213).

Questions

1. How did John Lewis, with great collaborative support, accomplish so much and be so grounded?

2. What are the risks and rewards of acting on the phrase, "Make strong trouble?" Journal.

"A Letter from a Birmingham Jail." April 12, 1963

HEADLINE from the BIRMINGHAM NEWS. "White Clergy Urge Local Negroes to Withdraw from Demonstrations." Eight prominent white, Southern clergy leaders challenged Dr. King's tactics in the highly charged Birmingham encounters of 1963 (Branch, WATERS 804).

His response to the white clergy was a "Letter" written on the margins of the BIRMINGHAM NEWS that was smuggled into his jail cell. It took about one month after Dr. King's release from jail on April 20 for the national media to realize the significance of King's "Letter from a Birmingham Jail" (Branch, WATERS 804). Among the many memorable passages of the epistle were King's "injustice anywhere is a threat to justice everywhere." According to King, his conceptual footing was grounded in God-given rights and the U.S. Constitution (Branch, PILLAR 46-48).

The local white clergy believed that King's demonstrations were poorly timed, pushing too fast, and creating "tensions" in the Birmingham community. Following are excerpts from the responses in his "letter."

Frankly I have yet to engage in a direct-action campaign that was "well-timed in view of those who have not suffered unduly form the disease of segregation...This "Wait" has always meant "Never."

Non-violent direct action seeks to create such a crisis and foster such a tension that a community that has constantly refused to negotiate is forced to confront the issue...(I)t can no longer be ignored...I am not afraid of the word "tension." I have earnestly opposed violent tension but there is a type of constructive non-violence that is necessary for growth. The question is not whether we will be extremists, but what kind of extremists we will be. Will we be extremists for hate or love? Will we be extremist for the preservation of injustice or for the extension of justice? (Abernathy 254-256).

President Kennedy sent troops to quell the bombings, dangerous use of fire hoses, and the accruing violence against Blacks in Birmingham. And with recent local political changes, the Alabama Supreme Court validated the election of a new Mayor Albert Boutwell and council members. Even Commissioner Bull Connor and other local hard-core, provocative leaders were displaced just before the Court action. Corporate outlets and local business leaders saw their numbers and profits diminishing from crucial boycotts and demonstrations (Abernathy 269).

The new city leaders, though not integrationists, set up bi-racial committees that ended in a mass change for Blacks, and reluctant desegregation for the city's whites. Within three days after the end of demonstrations, fitting rooms were desegrated. Within 30 days, city government officials set up court-ordered removal of signs in restrooms and drinking fountains. In 60 days, court-ordered lunch-room counters were desegregated. And within 15 days, new desegregated employment opportunities were established (Abernathy 268-269). The cracking walls of segregation continued.

"After the Birmingham settlement of May 10, an avalanche of Movement stories pictured the results by a government statistician... 758 racial demonstrations, 14,733 arrests in 186 cities, and the next ten weeks dramatized the countrywide Movement" (Branch, PILLARS 84).

Letter-Writing Exercise

The following letter-writing project is an outlet for analyzing what readers understand about Birmingham. This writing project will be a present-day approach to addressing any issue of consequence by the reader.

Based on the three, clustered statements from the Birmingham clergy articulated in Dr. King's "Letter," the reader will write a current letter on any crucial concern that utilizes his three responses about timing, speed, and tension/extremism. (See the above information from Dr. King.) Include in your argument timing, speed, and tension/extremism. The reader may choose a group or person to whom your current letter could be received.

Be free to discuss with others the main ideas and/or development of your letter. All letters count and matter, even with time delays and being significantly heard.

Questions

1. Was this Birmingham "Letter" the most important document of the Civil Rights era or was it like a modern piece of Christian, New Testament literature? Comment.

2. What was important about the ideas by the white clergy of timing, speed, and tension/extremism needing specific clarification by King?

3. What did the media information provide for the community?

4. What key factors contributed to the changes in Birmingham?

Wrap Up and Stories

Journaling Your Story

1. What are personal thoughts and feelings which develop for you in this chapter?

2. What changes may have occurred for you after addressing this chapter?

3. What personal insights and actions from this chapter may be applied to your everyday experiences?

Conclusion

In conclusion, we have discussed the nature of social relationships for social change. From an abstract recognition of all change as inevitable, we have charted the move from passive toward active engagement.

Also, we may be infused with intentionality. Because of increased participation, understanding and peer influence, we can be enriched or demoralized by our acceptance of and emotional attachment to social change.

Often our connections to a social movement develop from attention to issues and to our personal associations with persons directly engaged in social change. We may even express compassion toward persons entrenched in what we perceive as relatively negative social change. This may be a healthy test of our compassion, commitment and chance for growth.

Maturity in our social relationships may shift from superficiality to in-depth connections, from caution to risk-taking, from detachment to full inclusion. All of this may happen whether or not we are courageous followers or leaders.

Questions

1. Does it take more than protestors and government to bring about social change? Explain.

2. Discuss the roles of leaders and followers in attempting social change.

3. What central lessons are derived from engaging with the information in this chapter?

4. Do you believe that much of the information in this chapter is largely unknown? Explain.

Works Cited

Abernathy, Ralph David. AND THE WALLS CAME TUBBLING DOWN. Harper and Row, 1989, pp. 254-256.

Alonso, Paola. "Autonomy Revoked: The Forced Sterilization of Women of Color in 20th Century America." Article from TEXAS WOMAN'S UNIVERSITY, 2019, p. 1

Branch, Taylor. PARTING THE WATERS: AMERICA IN THE KING YEARS 1954-1963. Simon and Schuster, 1988, p. 804.

—, PILLAR OF FIRE: AMERICA IN THE KING YEARS 1963-1965. Simon and Schuster, 1998, pp. 46-48, 84.

Change, Ailsa. "All Things Considered," NPR, 29 June 2022.

Clark, Septima. "Finding Your Way Back Home." REFUSE TO STAND BY, edited by Eliot Wigginton, Doubleday, 1991, pp. 232, 236, 240.

Evans, Christopher. THE SOCIAL GOSPEL IN AMERICAN RELIGION. New York University Press, 2017, p. 46.

Farmer, James. LAY BARE THE HEART: AN AUTOBIOGRAPHY OF THE CIVIL RIGHTS MOVEMENT. New American Library, 1985, p. 213.

Grose, Charles. Walter Mondale speech on the 1964 Democratic Convention about Experiences Surrounding the Credentials Committee at Minneapolis, Ted Mann Concert Hall, 2005.

—, Interview of Yale student, New Haven, 1961.

Haagland, Deb. PBS News, 16 July 2021.

Kaelber, Lutz. "Eugenics: Compulsory Sterilization in 50 States." Presentation at the Social Science History Association in Vermont, 2012, p. 1.

Lewis, Wesley and Andrew Pauwels, Brian Underwood, and Andrianna Rodriguez. "John Lewis: Profile of Civil Rights Legend," ABA, 22 Jan. 2021.

Lindsay, Willian. "Social Movement and Feminism." University of Chicago Press, American Journal of Theology and Philosophy, Vol 13, No 3, Sep. 1992, pp. 206-208.

Manjeshwar, Sanjana. "America's Forgotten History of Forced Sterilization." BERKELEY POLITICAL REVIEW, pp. 1-3.

Medosch, Emily. "No Just ICE: Forced Sterilization in the United States." HUMAN RIGHTS LAW REVIEW, 28 May 2021.

Newland, Bryan. "Federal Boarding Schools Initiative Investigative Report." DOI, INDIAN AFFAIRS, May 2022, pp. 12, 92-95.

News and Commentary. "Immigration Detention and Coerced Sterilization: History Tragically Repeated Itself." ACLU, 29 Sep. 2020, pp. 2-4.

Parks, Rosa. "Sitting at the Back of the Bus When It Was Already Crowded." REFUSE TO STAND BY, edited by Eliot Wigginton, Doubleday, 1991, pp. 232-234, 236, 240.

Schaefer, Richard. RACIAL AND ETHNIC GROUPS. New Jersey, Upper Saddle River, 2020, p. 162.

Spann, J. Richard (ed). THE CHURCH AND SOCIAL RESPONSIBILITY. Abington Press Cokesbury, 1953, p. 21.

Specia, Megan. "Overlooked No More: Cary Shook Up the Abolitionist Movement." Obituary, NYT, 6 June 2018.

Staples, Brent. Editorial. NYT, Sunday Review, 28 June 2018, p. SR4.

Stern, Alexandra Minna. "Forced Sterilization Policies int the U.S. Targeted Minorities and Those with Disabilities - and Lasted Until the 21st Century." MICHIGAN INSTITUTE FOR HEALCARE POLICY AND INNOVATION, 3 Sep. 2020.

U.S. Department of Interior. "Releases Investigative Report, Outlines Next Steps in Federal Indian Boarding School Initiative." 11 May 2022.

Watkins, Valethia. "Votes for Women: Race, Gender and W.E.B. Du Bois' Advocacy for Women's Suffrage." PHYLON, Clarke University Press, Vol 53, No 2, Winter 2016, pp. 16-19.

Winfield, Nicole and Peter Smith. "Pope Apologizes for 'Catastrophic' School Policy in Canada." Associated Press News, 26 June 2022.

Zinn, Howard. SNNC: THE NEW ABOLITIONISTS. Boston, Beacon Press, 1965, pp. 251-255, 261.

Chapter 7

Current Social Movements
for Social Change

"Beyond individual cases comes the need for something broader...in this transformative era. We are all being carried along on a river of change," declared Angela Davis (Solnit 4SR). Do we flow aimlessly downstream or choose to go courageously upstream? Davis adapted the classic "Serenity Prayer." "I am no longer accepting the things I cannot change. I am changing the things I cannot accept" (Lightsey).

Introduction

Social changes are essential to each day's interactions just as our natural world inherently changes.

Racial differences challenge us to deepen, empower and accept those differences as we are impacted by personal and social changes. More specifically, our racial relations were created and experienced by the power of change indirectly and directly.

Movement insiders feel the empowerment, frustration and disappointment of participation within a social movement where "success" is often illusive and slow to achieve. Social movements are very personal and dynamic.

We are reminded that a "social movement is an ongoing, goal-directed effort to fundamentally challenge social institutions, attitudes or ways of life" (Brinkerhoff et al. 424). The current social movements in the United States include animal rights, environmental, #METOO, gun violence and gun reform, LGBTQ, feminist/pro-choice, pro-life, law enforcement, sanctuary, campus movements and numerous others.

Gun Violence and Parkland Students' Creation of the
"March for our Lives Movement"

Ravaging a school, redeeming its suffering - Marjory Stoneman Douglass High School, Parkland, Florida

How has the 2018 Parkland massacre been different for its high-school students and the country? A lone white male with a semiautomatic rifle sprayed bullets inside the high school for barely six minutes and 20 seconds. Seventeen people, mostly students, were slaughtered and many more injured (Walsh 6).

Shooters can be neighbors and community members who are usually young men, ages 18-20. They give warnings. They have their own way of "crying out for help," states criminologist Dr. Julian Peterson. Many mass shooters face "isolation, racism, misogyny, violence, gun access, and social media screeds," declared Professor Snyder (Snyder SR6).

Questions

1. What are the general characteristics of a mass-violence shooter?

2. How could empathy be expressed for those connected to the Parkland tragedy?

Marching for Our Lives in D.C. Led by Parkland Students

What astounding vision and coordination resulted in the Parkland, student-led "March for Our Lives" in Washington D. C. only five weeks after the Parkland massacre (Shear 1, 22). Estimates of tens of thousands to several-hundred thousand persons came to give voice to their cause of gun-laws reform (Shear 1).

The June 11, 2018, March for Our Lives rally in Washington, D. C., was spearheaded by Parkland co- founders X Gonzalez and David Hogg. In her animated speech to Congress, Gonzalez declared, "We are the children to do the heavy lifting for you...You are not elected to make decisions for us. You are elected to pass our will into law" (CSpan 6.12.22). Hogg's speech affirmed, "All of us do agree, left and right, gun owners and non-gun owners, that we must take action to save lives now" (LeBlanc and Fortinsky 2022). Think about what was said in Parkland just after the 2018 mass shooting. The survivors "delivered a resounding message that Washington's inaction on the scourge of gun violence is no longer acceptable" (LeBlanc and Fortinsky 22). Seas of signs flooded the D. C. Mall and side streets as tightly-packed advocates marched. A sample of the signs read "Protect Kids Not Guns," "Be the Change," "NRA Kills," "Never Again," "Disarm the Police," "Black Lives Matter," and "We Call BS, Enough Is Enough" (Shear 22-23).

Questions

1. What is behind the leadership of Hogg and Gonzalez's commitment to the movement?

2. What key parts of their messages resonate for you?

3. What angles of their speeches might have stimulated Congress to action?

For some, inspiration was a consequence of students' speaking with poise and maturity (Shear 22). Parkland student Emma Gonzalez told reporters, "We could very well die trying to do this. But we could very well die not trying to do this. So why not die for something rather than nothing?" (Walsh 6). She stunned the event after reading the names of the 17 student victims with uncomfortable silence. When Gonzalez broke the silence at the microphone, she said, "Since the time I came out here, it has been six minutes and 20 seconds...Fight for your lives before it's someone else's job" (Walsh 6). Jacelyn Corin said with empathy, "We share the stage with communities who have always stared down the barrels of guns" (CNN 2018). An 11-year-old student, Naomi Wadler, said, "Never again," in support of Black girls and women who have experienced gun violence (Shear 22). Popular singers and students boldly communicated their fears and hopes for change (CSPAN 2018).

Questions

1. What do you think about Gonzalez's time for silence in her speech?

2. How do you evaluate the tactics included in the Rally?

3. What could this activism by Latina students mean for Latinos elsewhere?

Dave Cullen, author of the Columbine killings, perceived that the D. C. March was "completely different...This isn't about just grief, horror, pain and sadness. This is about doing something" (Walsh 6-7). And another special insight was from Parkland students as stated by journalist Joan Walsh. They "endeavored to meld their cause to the cause of young black people, who disproportionately suffer from gun violence" (Walsh 7). A Parkland resident at the Washington rally said that "these leaders are children...but they've lost their childhood" (Walsh 7). Numerous students of diverse ages at the March forcefully articulated that they are eager to vote in this fall's elections or in several years (Shear 22). Overall, it can be said that the Parkland students, and others, are moving from reaction to pro-action, from agony to empowerment, and from being ravaged to discovering redemption in suffering.

1. What made this March different? Journal.

2. What could be the roles of the Parkland March for people of color generally?

I met David Hogg in Minneapolis. At a public event, he remarked about an open-session question. "Aren't you young people the ones to carry forward the cause of gun control?" Hogg's response was, "It will take all of us to work on gun violence" (Grose 2020).

Opposition to the D. C. Gun Safety Rally

Small rallies for the Second Amendment happened in cities like Salt Lake City, Phoenix and Boston (Turkewitz 23). Some of the participants spoke of March for Our Lives types as "ignorant of the Constitution, ...not true Americans" (Turkewitz 23). One participant would consider compromising. To stop mass shootings, one sign at a demonstration said, "Shoot Back" (Turkewitz 23). Some signs in Salt Lake City declared, "AR 15's Empower the People" (Shear 22).

Questions

1. What is it about high school students which motivates them recently to act on gun safety?

2. What were possible motives of the opposition at the Washington rally?

Further understand the immense impact of the March for Our Lives. On TV talk shows, students opened up for the world to hear ("AM Joy" 2018). Rallies against gun violence occurred in "390 of the country's 435 congressional districts" (Shear 22). Country-wide, anticipated rallies were scheduled in at least 400 cities in approximately 50 states that weekend according to CNN (LeBlanc and Fortinsky 12.6.22). Worldwide, there were at least 800 "sibling rallies" (CSPAN 2018).

Question

Explore the potential impact of widespread, supportive events from the March for Our Lives?

From 2019 - 2021, gun deaths rose by 30% (Mistry and Raddaz 2022).

Question

What do you think are reasons for increases in gun deaths?

Black Lives Matter Movement

A spark that fueled the fires of a current social movement is Black Lives Matter, BLM. Three geographically- distant community organizers felt the pain, frustration and anger over the killing of Trayvon Martin in August, 2013. Deeply touched, Alicia Garza and her companion activists, Patrisse Cullors and Opal Tometi, helped popularize the phrase #Black Lives Matter as a hashtag on Twitter and Tumble. (Baptiste 35) From these extraordinary circumstances, that social movement was born (Guynn B3).

Questions

1. What do you think about the power of an idea to help create a movement?

2. What emotions and skills of community organizers may contribute to the rise of this movement?

#blacklivesmatter.org is the new organization which supports the social movement. The organization "is an online forum intended to build connections between Black people and our allies to fight anti-Black racism, to spark a dialogue among Black people, and to facilitate the types of connections necessary to encourage social action and engagement" (BLACK LIVES MATTER).

Developing Pattern of a "Leaderful" Movement

Differing from the Civil Rights Movement that was largely led by a small group of leaders of Black organizations, BLM is extraordinarily leaderful. There is apparently little hierarchy in this movement of countless leaders. This "leaderful" movement is demonstrated by Johnetta Elzie and DeRay McKesson. They marched through American cities while texting, as charge cords and battery packs fall out of...pockets." They would "tweet a time and location, and then wait for the people to show up." (Kang 36). Another local leader who helped guide the Minneapolis chapter even before the George Floyd lynching is the lawyer, activist Nekima Levy Armstrong (Grose).

Question

What are the strengths and weaknesses of a "leaderful" Movement?

Individual Activists

Among the BLM activists are young adults, the megaphone leader of event chants, along with the hair-colored young women who may be present with her male/female companion. Astonishing are the stroller-pushing parents who may bring one or more of their youngsters. And middle-aged men and women keep up with the other activists. Not to be excluded are the white-haired, perennial activists who inspire others just by being there. As this movement progresses, so does the number of committed core persons.

Questions

1. What key factors contributed to the rising from grassroots actions to this social movement?

2. How would you characterize the individual activists?

Eight-Stage Process of Moyer

Be intrigued by the vital, innovative eight-stage process for social movements invented by the late, nonviolent activist and scholar Bill Moyer. Those stages are "normal times," "prove the failures of official institutions," "ripening conditions," "take off," "perception of failure," "majority public opinion," "success," and "continuing the struggle" (Moyer 130-228).

Stage VI - Majority Public Opinion (in Moyer's framework of movements)

It seems that The Black Lives Matter Movement has moved into Stage VI - Majority Public Opinion. The movement's goal is to be nurturing and energizing the power of grassroot individuals and groups. From spontaneous, short-term crisis protests, the movement must be consciously transformed for its long-phased development. Winning over a larger proportion of the movement's populace complements the acceptance of the movement's positions by a great majority of powerholders, the non-political population and mainstream elected politicians. Therefore, these movement activists are primed to wage their own strategy for the upcoming Stage VII when the majority is winning social change against the powerholders (Moyer 64-75).

Action

A mini or ongoing observation of a BLM event is appropriate to more fully understand what the actions are and what they mean. (I heard from a local TV announcement and quickly joined the event.) You can find a movement event from the media or hearing about it from friends. Often these events are at public buildings like the state capitol or the county-court house or the city center.

Below are the characteristics in this Stage VI.

Stage VI - Majority Public Opinion

Mainstream citizens and institutions are involved in addressing the problem.

It is shown how the problem and policies affect all sectors of society.

Problem attention is put on the political agenda.

Majority opposes present conditions and powerholder policies.

Current actions counter each new powerholder's strategy.

Alternatives are promoted.

Powerholders encourage the public's fear of alternatives and activism.

Enhancing a paradigm shift (tradition), not just reforms, becomes secure.

Trigger events like those of Stage IV's "Take-Off are re-enacted for a short period. (Moyer 45).

Overall, The Black Lives Matter Movement has gained stature, visibility, sustainability and mainstream recognition. This is now more than the take-off stage for the movement that began seven years ago (Grose).

Shift in BLM Impact

A real shift in the Black Lives Matter's influence has happened by effective action for racial fairness.

Corporations have changed branding that re-enforces racial stereotypes. Cities have removed statues of racists. Schools have disconnected ties with police forces. Cities have reduced police funding. And people with power have been educating themselves and the public about the role of social movements to achieve change (Hunter SR3).

Importantly, the media were immersed in the visual trauma of the protests, which ended up in Washington, D. C. Eventually, a main street in the Capitol had large-lettered Black Lives Matter letters painted on the pavement. Buildings have the BLM letters painted on them. Hunter says that social movements also alter the terrain on which power players are changed as they face voting issues (Hunter SR3). When Abram X. Kendi became the director of Boston University's new racial research center in 2021, he recognized the nationwide urgency of the movement. Across every segment of society, he now sees "growing support for the Black Lives Matter movement, and racial equity" (Rimer 56).

Questions

1. Comment briefly on Stage VI as a whole.

2. We are challenged to evaluate whether or not the Movement's recent successes suitably reflect the characteristics/criteria for Stage VI. Journal.

3. Why are many whites reluctant to appreciate the non-violence of the Movement?

4. Why have other racial groups not picked up on using their name with............Matter?

George Floyd and the Law Enforcement Change Movement

According to the Minneapolis police press release, "Man dies after medical incident during police interaction" (web.archive.org, 25 May 2020).

The reader may refer to the entire, original police press release following that dramatic event. ("Investigative Update on Critical Incident." 26 May 2020).

What do you think could be missing from the original Minneapolis police report by the officers engaged in the Floyd murder? Below see other components that could have been a part of the report.

Early on, while Floyd was still in his car with no apparent gun, an officer pointed a gun at him.

Absent was the notation about restraining Mr. Floyd on the pavement.

No indication was given of an officer holding his knee on Floyd's neck for nine minutes and 29 seconds.

Floyd repeatedly declared, "I can't breathe. I can't breathe."

Before Floyd lost consciousness, he kept calling out for his "mama."

He lost his pulse.

Office Chauvin remained on Floyd's neck until paramedics told Chauvin to completely get off of Floyd's body.

An off-duty firefighter was rebuffed when attempting to provide aid for Floyd.

A major gap of about 20 minutes in the report ignores what police did at the event (Levenson 2022).

Questions

1. How aware is the public about the incomplete reporting by the police on these kinds of crucial events?

2. What can be done to change these types of incomplete initial reporting by the police?

3. What are your thoughts about the avoidance of attention to Floyd's life/death medical needs?

A deep payback for Floyd's death resulted in massive protests, including those of BLM, that began on the streets of Minneapolis and St. Paul beginning May 25, 2022. Worldwide protests were covered.

What makes this social change movement different? 1. The **police** officers have been **imprisoned** for the murder of one unarmed-black man that sparked immense social **change.** 2. **Numbers.** Several hundred-thousand protestors have engaged in action across our country. 3. **Persons of every stripe** are included in each of the demonstrations. These diverse crowds included mostly non-violent activists and some rioters. It was the violent rioters who caused the vandalism, fires and property destruction. 4. Strikingly, **international** responses to embedded injustices also have now become glaring. 5. Even a deep-seated **shift** among **whites** has surfaced as they are increasingly persuaded by the reality of racism. 6. And, the **speed** at which **governmental institutions** have responded with **structural change** initiatives is remarkable. The Minneapolis City Council has voted to reform its police force. And the governor has engaged the State Human Rights Department which has already taken strategic actions. In Houston, Texas, the mayor has issued executive orders to eliminate police chokeholds/neck force and focus on de-escalation tactics. 7. White **nationalists, hate groups and anarchists** have significantly distracted persons while bringing violent fear and local **property destruction** to marches. A few extremists have been located who had confused the media and others about their identity in the protest marches. 8. The **media, diverse institutions and families** continue to be struck by in-depth **conversations** about recent crimes against unarmed innocent Black persons. 9. Remarkably, many professional **athletes, their owners** and others are **donating** large sums of money to support vulnerable persons in these times of upheaval (Grose).

What are the official results of a study of police events surrounding the murder of George Floyd? The Minnesota Human Rights Commission recently reported on the actions and inactions regarding the interactions between Minneapolis police and George Floyd. Of the major criticisms of the local police, the report stipulates police discrimination and use of excessive force. Beyond choke holds and knee-on-neck actions, inadequate police training and lack of attention to medical treatment are documented (Mannix and Navratil 7).

Progress on a long-standing memorial for George Floyd is developing at the intersection of 38th street and Chicago and has been re-designed in Minneapolis. "The intersection's chief occupation now is the focal point of a social movement," asserts the April 30 editorial of the Star Tribune newspaper. It hopes that "the grassroots spirit of the George Floyd Square" will remain in its "artwork, giant fists and the names of many Black people killed in encounters with police...People have inscribed slogans, biblical quotes, calls to action, demands for justice and names." These items are displayed on "cardboard, concrete slabs of wood, and walls on buildings" for impassioned residents and thousands of visitors (Editorial 30 May 2022). I watched the officer's knee-on-the neck violence at the time it occurred, and the trial on TV.

Questions

1. What do you think would be a creative kind of memorial for George Floyd? Consider a broad array of long-lasting items and their symbolic strength. High-held fists mark the intersections one block in each direction of Floyd's death, and another huge fist at 38th and Chicago. At that intersection, an African American flag of red, black, and green stripes is held high above the fist.

2. Comment on my facts about what makes the Floyd events different and widespread.

3. Do you think that justice for Floyd's family and the officers will be a model for other police abuse? Explain.

4. Why do you consider that social movements are vital to bringing about social change?

Think about the recent tragic murder of another Black man and blatant undisciplined violence by police, and fire departments in Memphis. Black adult, Tyre Nichols, was murdered by Black police officers while under suspicion of reckless driving in Memphis. Tennessee, on January 7, 2023. The five officers were fired, two others suspended, and two EMT technicians and a fire department lieutenant were suspended (Patil 2023). "It's not racism driving this, it's culturalism," said Robert Sausedo, the head of a Los Angeles non-profit research group. Others have declared "that problems of race and policing are a function of an entrenched police culture of aggression and dehumanization of Black people more than of interpersonal racism" (McGrady 1).

1. Does the deadly violence by Black officers make a difference in your thoughts about the event? Explain.

2. What do you say about the understanding that the issue again is about the police culture of violence generally? Journal.

Recent Student Activism

The hidden power of college students can be supercharged with courage, curiosity and high expectations. Raw numbers and potential force are tempered by their liberal arts education that highlights critical thinking and humane values. Crucial to the enlightened goals of this type of education are the captivating actions and enriched rewards from service learning and collegial community development. Colleges are wise and creative as they encourage student activism.

Activism of this type leads to questions about what motivates students.

1. Social motives help prevent student loneliness which continues to be a chronic issue.

2. Respect from friends is also an initiator for student engagement. Personal idols and community support strengthen involvement.

3. Students are urged to participate in part because it encourages personal development and the exercise of power.

4. Benefits from activism include appreciation from allies and other significant others. Plus, skills are gained that are not provided in the college curriculum.

5. And activism may occur by coincidence and for some it becomes a lifestyle.

6. Even university administrators are coming to recognize and understand the value of student activism (Ansala et al. 152).

Activism helps develop communication skills, connective relation-building, and critical thinking.

"We need new ways to approach citizenship because society necessitate it." In an effort to create a more equitable world, students presently draw on courses and campus institutions observed Charles Henebray of Boston University (Bouranova 14).

Today's "activists treat the university as an ally, not an opponent," says Henebray (Bouranova 14-16). Outreach activities have engaged students in "hood renovationz" such as free remodeling of homes, and community youth centers, says activist Daisy Figueroa. A Black BU organization invites other campus groups like Black sister groups, and "anyone connected to the cause," says their leader, Derrick Luther. "Students of color don't feel valued and affirmed, and they don't feel they can be their true authentic selves," stipulates President Lori White of DePauw University. A new, 70-member college organization called Liberal Arts Leaders Alliance for Racial Equity, LALARE, has been initiated by President White (Dieter 1). Other causes include gun control, climate change, transgender rights and racial justice. (Bouranova 16).

And there is a surge of high-school activism that some have not seen since the 1960s. This type of civic engagement is "developmentally appropriate for students of this age," references Christine Fernando (Fernando 5).

College students still participate in protests in student movements at a 20% rate during the current epidemic. And, 57% articulate that they are currently more likely to discuss race. Plus, 60% of white peers in this 2021 Student Voice Survey declared that race comes up more frequently in discussions. This sample included about 1,100 white students and about 800 students of color (Ezarik Racial Justice).

Questions

1. How do you as a reader respond to this information about student activism?

2. What do you think stimulates university administrators to be more compatible with student activism?

3. What do you say about the idea that change necessitates both voting and protests? Journal.

Readers may Change through Normalized and Non-Normalized Processes

Normalized Process

This normalized process can be enacted with any person and with any group. According to authors Jodi Pfarr and Allison Boisvert.

Out societal system regularly normalizes one particular thing over another...When one group has all four components (individuals, organizations, communities, and policies) geared toward it, that group will receive inherent benefits...When something becomes normalized, the social system creates supports for that which has become normalized (Pfarr and Boisvert 25-57).

Right-handed persons are normalized and are not to blame for being that way as are left-handed persons who are non-normalized (Pfarr and Boisvert 26).

Non-normalized Process

Non-normalized persons do not get the benefits and positive experiences of persons who are normalized. And there is a power discrepancy for us who are non-normalized (Pfarr and Boisvert 26). An example of this difference in power can be applied to people of color who are non-normalized.

Many of us are intrigued by pursuing the process known as normalization in our societal system. Jodi Pfarr articulates that the normalization/non-normalization process is geared toward a specific group, or for our purposes a particular race. Her example is that of South Africa. Even though for many years of apartheid, the white minority population gained and held normalized control of the Country. That was due to the preferential treatment allowed whites within national policies and practices. After the apartheid ended in 1993, policies and practices dramatically changed. Yet, with the higher standard of living, wages, and owning much more land, the white population continued to hold crucial power and remained dominant or normalized. Normalization can be slow to change (Pfarr and Boisvert 28-29).

Individual Paired Actions

So where do we go from here as a reader? You may look at the paired items that are below. In everyday conversation and contact, our interactions may be better clarified as we understand the succeeding columns of pairs. Those paired items guide our thinking, emotions and actions about what is normal and non-normal in our society (Pfarr and Boisvert 28). More than 100 Mayflower UCC members individually discussed their idea of pairs in small groups led by Pfarr in 2022 at the Minneapolis church (Grose 2022).

When you consider the idea of two contrasting groups, you can begin addressing the paired scheme. Each pair represents two items in a group. "A triangle pointing down represents a group that is not normalized...A triangle pointing up is labeled a group that is normalized" (Pfarr and Boisvert 29). Yet for our purposes, we use pairs of differing groups rather than triangles.

Look below at items organized under Normalized versus Non-Normalized.

When we accept how the paired items do exist and specifically identify them for our lives, then we can understand how it impacts us, our loved ones and co-workers. After using how the racial naming experience exists for us, we may talk about the experience with others and in small groups.

Normalized	Non-Normalized
Euro Ethnicity	Other Ethnicity
White	People of Color
White	Latinos
White	Asian American
White	American Indian
White	African American
White	Mixed Race

Exercise when choosing Normalized versus Non-Normalized experiences

Above, picture circling only one of the two items in each pair or otherwise identifying it. For example, we could choose or circle us right-hand persons under Normalized and us left-handed persons under Non-Normalized.

1. Start with your **general viewpoint** of groups. Select those with either Euro-Ethnic origins contrasted with groups showing Other Ethnic backgrounds. Which one did you circle or pick? What does this suggest to you about understanding racial differences?

2. In the next Normalized and Non-normalized pair, what did you select in terms of **general race relations** (White or People of Color)? How did you feel about identifying with only one of those two broad racial items? Journal.

3. In the above **specific racial pairs**, proceed to go down the columns and choose one item within each pair. Do you see the individual racial group as non-normalized or normalized? What are your feelings about your racial responses? No answer is right or wrong. Are your thoughts different when contrasting each dominant group with each separate racial group (Asian or Latino) or …? Reflect on your way of relating to racial groups. Explain.

4. Practice with examples. Using the Normalized versus Non-Normalized scheme, what might you identify about the constituents of a workforce, school classroom, etc. setting? Your responses?

5. Our next involvement means working within **real situations**. Find a small group, and discuss the situation so far with openness and candor. How may you feel about not identifying with one Normalized or Non-Normalized racial individual? Journal.

6. As you count the number of items you identified in the overall process, how do you feel about being in a few of the items or almost all of the items in a column? What do you think about identifying with a dominant column or a person-of-color column? Explain.

Active Endings and My Story

Pulling together your reader's stories is vital to grappling with this chapter on social movements. As you consider your responses to the experience with this chapter, it is essential to articulate your usual four approaches to your encounter with this chapter. This again becomes your story from this chapter.

Journal with as much depth as possible your **thoughts, feelings,** and any **changes** which occurred from your engagement with the contents and methods about social movements. And describe how elements of this chapter relate to **everyday life.**

Conclusion

The latent power of African Americans, gun violence reformers, and students, has re-awakened and mobilized many of us for racial social change. Our collective actions even make incremental differences.

Works Cited

Alexander, Michelle. "How to Dismantle the 'New Jim Crow." SOJOURNERS, 14 July 2014, p. 18.

Ansala, Liisa, and Sato Uusiautti, and Karina Maatta. "What are Students Motives for Participating in Student Activism?" INTRODUCTORY JOURNAL OF ADOLESCENCE AND YOUTH, Vol 21, Issue 2, 2 Apr. 2016.

Baptiste, Nathalie. "Origins of a Movement." NATION, 27 Feb. 2017, p. 35.

BLACK LIVES MATTER

Brinkerhoff, David. ESSENTIALS OF SOCIOLOGY. Wadsworth Publishers, 2002, p. 424.

Bouranova, Alene. "Rising Up." BOSTONIA, 26 Mar. 2021, pp. 14-16.

CSpan, 12 June 2022.

Dieter, Mary. "DePauw Stories." 11 November, 2020, p. 1.

Dickerson, John. CBS, Sunday Morning Show, 12 June 2022.

Editorial STAR TRIBUNE, 4 May 2022, p.6.

Ezarik, Melissa. "More discussion than Action: Racial Justice on Campus." INSIDE HIGHER EDUCATION, 6 May 2021.

Fernando, Christine. "This is American: Amid a Surge in Student Activism, We Need to Respect the Voices of Young People." USA Today, 20 Jan. 2022, p. 5.

Grose, Charles. Information from actions as a participant in the awareness process, Minneapolis, 2022.

Hunter, Daniel. "Don't Believe the Lie That Voting Is All You Can Do." NYT, Opinion, 4 Aug. 2020.

LeBlanc, Paul and Sarah Fortinsky. "Student-led March for Our Lives Rally Pushed for Action on Gun Violence." CNN, Washington, 12 June 2022.

Levenson, Eric. CNN, 24 Apr. 2022.

Lightsey, Pamala. "Today's Activists Protest Oppression with a New Prophetic Power." FOCUS MAGAZINE, Spring 2016.

Mannix, Andy and Liz Navratil. "Dept. of Human Rights Report on Minneapolis Police. STAR TRIBUNE, 2 Apr. 2022, p. 7.

McGrady, Clyde. "Officers' Race Turns Focus to System." NYT, 29 Jan. 2023, p. 1.

Mistry, Began and Martha Raddaz. "Sandy Hook Survivors Speaker Out for the First Time - and Share Their Heartache." ABC, This Week with George Stephenopoulos, 12 June 2022.

Mover, Bill. "Doing Democracy." NEW SOCIETY PUBLISHERS, 2001, pp. 130-228.

Patil, Aushka. "Here Is a Timeline of Events in the Death of Tyre Nichols." NYT, 26 Jan. 2023.

Pfarr, Jodie and Allison Boisvert. THE URGENCY OF AWARENESS. MCP Books, 2019, pp. 28-42.

Rimer, Sara. "In June, Just Weeks after George Floyd was Killed." BOSTONIA, Spring, 2020, p. 56.

Solnit, Rebecca. "Don't Stop Believing That People Can Change." NYT, 24 Apr. 2022, p. SR4.

Snyder, Rachael. "The Most Dangerous Years." NYT, Week in Review, 12 June 2022, p. SR6.

web.archive.org, 25 May 2020.

Chapter 8

How Many Ways Can We Undo Race
and Racism?

"In short, a candid examination of race matters takes us to the core of the crisis of American democracy" (West 156).

When exploring an over-arching framework for this chapter, we connect our current experiences, perspectives, empathy, and their application to present life. Delicate relationships and uncertain outcomes are illuminated. Any of the frameworks and approaches in this chapter can be implemented to creatively and boldly confront any racial actions. And all the previous parts of this book provide contextual content and adaptable methods from which you may innovatively build in this action-filled chapter. Be enriched and share with others.

High school students and adults still explore racism using the Moving Walkway created originally by Dr. Beverly Tatum. It's a conversation opener.

Moving Walkway and Dealing with Racism

>>

1. Running with the walkway – Active white supremacist.

2. Walking with the walkway – Entitled to say or do any racist thing anywhere, anytime I like it.

3. Occasionally stepping with the walkway – "I'm not a racist but..."

4. Standing still – a. Seeing ourselves as "good people." b. Saying, "I can't be racist since I've adopted two children of color." c. Don't know what I don't know.

5. Turned around and standing still – A little information, a little action, and yet face oncoming racism with inaction. "I tried to fight racism at my kid's school once and it just didn't work."

6. Occasionally stepping against the walkway – Maybe interrupting a joke, challenging a comment, or educating someone else.

7. Walking against the walkway – Challenging racism on a daily/ regular basis.

8. Running against the walkway – Challenging white privilege/white supremacy on a regular basis. (Hackman adapted)

How do we see ourselves on a particular status of the walkway?

In what ways might we want to change our location on the walkway? Explain.

A Guided Framework to Uproot Race and Racism

This framework can be universally useful for organizing descriptions and analyses of individual and group situations of race. All topics can be adapted.

1. History/Context

2. Awareness of the Issue

3. Awakening to the Issue

4. Proaction by Groups and Individuals

5. Coalition Building

6. Action Consequences

7. Continuing Commitments

8. New and Revised Decisions and Actions

A vital, recent illustration of actions to eradicate the system of race and racial hierarchy in Dallas is framed within the above Guided Framework.

History/Context. "Y'all" is a warm, welcoming greeting in Dallas, Texas. It is the emotional frontier of the South before entering Western Texas. Dallas is a conservative city of over one million population.

For centuries the tribal federation of the Caddo, the Comanche and Creek tribes lived in what is now Dallas. The Caddo, for example, were forcefully removed in 1858 to what is now Oklahoma in accordance with the 1830 Indian Removal Act (Minutes UT 1969).

A profoundly consequential event in Dallas was the assassination of President J. F. Kennedy in 1963. And in the summer of 2016, a Black veteran killed five Dallas police officers and two civilians (McGhee 285).

Awareness of the Issue. For Black persons, there is perennial awareness. And for white persons, to be aware of the structured racial hierarchy is superficial at best.

Awakening of the Issue. Caught in the throes of a dynamic idea, we describe a brief portrait of racial change in Dallas. Black Dr. Gail Christopher moved beyond her awareness to a re-awakening about racial hierarchy. In the U.S., "We have never had a replacement of our system of racial hierarchy," she said. Strictly as humans, we need to envision an America that can bend the moral arc of the universe toward justice. Christopher pondered "What kind of a narrative will your great grand-children learn about this country?" (McGhee287).

Proaction. Called into action in Dallas to address Christopher's idea were 175 experts. They concluded that Dallas, and the U.S., need racial transformation.

Coalition Building. Civic leaders, business people, police officers, grassroots organizers, hundreds of students, and the overall public committed to a visioning process in small groups in public libraries. Within the opening pages of the finale bold report, it read that "DALLAS IS ON STOLEN LAND...DALLAS WAS BUILT WITH STOLEN LABOR (McGhee 285). (Small groups are considered coalitions for our purposes, but they are usually organizations who join together for common goals and impact.)

Action Consequences. That inter-racial visioning process engendered major change in Dallas. An inventive approach (HRHT) to enrich that change became the only overall organization in the City which focused on racial equity. (Oakland, California, has dozens of comparable organizations.) That organization is called the Truth, Racial Healing, and Transformation project, according to its staff leader, Jerry Hawkins. TRHT has become a model for challenging the racial hierarchy in terms of old laws, separation, and the economy. Organized narratives for change are addressing school curricula, the media and historic monuments (McGhee 282-283).

National consequences are identified:

After Dallas, fourteen U.S. communities launched HRHT efforts by 2017.

The American Association of Colleges and Universities facilitated 24 HRHT college centers by 2018.

And U.S. House Representative Barbara Lee introduced a "resolution urging the establishment of a TRHT Commission" in 2020 (McGhee 282).

Local Action Consequences

A conservative Dallas councilwoman worked to issue an official city proclamation to recognize HRHT.

The Dallas school district and the City developed new Offices of Racial Equity.

Through Jerry Hawkin's leadership in the County Historical Commission, he and his colleagues have trained high level City administrators about racial equity.

And Jerry has taught Southern Methodist University students about redlining, blockbusting, and encouraged their career plans to include restructuring equity in society (McGhee 285).

Continuing Commitments. Local efforts are attempting to mobilize the national government to support racial equity. Author McGhee raises this question for us all, "Who is an American, and what are we to one another?" So many differences force us to admit our common humanity (McGhee 288). The laws we have made are expressions of a deep-seated root of inequality. "The great lie at the root of our nation's founding was belief in the hierarchy of human value. And we are still there" (McGhee 288).

New and revised actions from the Dallas model could have been the last topic in our above Guided Framework.

Framework for Becoming an Anti-Racist Person or Group

What is a process for you or a group to become anti-racist? What does it mean to act as an ant-racist? A central ingredient in the process is the undergirding power expressed in all racial actions. Power is the ability to control decision-making. This succeeding framework is another approach to personally or institutionally confront racism. The list below shows descending **levels of power** for working through becoming anti-racist. (The reader may only choose to do any section, or all, of this Anti-Racist Framework, numbers 1.– 4.)

1. Identify the reader's choices below to scan one's own experience for at least a week. Journaling or using a computer spreadsheet would offer practical approaches for this part.

    a. Structural racism – firmly organized large-group actions with clear functions

    b. Institutional racism – policies that are overt, covert, indirect, subtle

    c. Individual racism – negative actions against alleged-subordinant persons

    d. White privilege – individual acts, controlled by the advantaged system

e. "Colorblind racism" – not seeing nor acknowledging color differences

f. Cultural racism – "meritocracy," accepting achievement "by your bootstraps"

g. Racial Microaggressions – unintentional, subtle actions

h. Minimalized racism – diminished expectations about persons of color

i. Laissez Faire – status quo without actions

2. What does it mean to be an **anti-racist group**? Address the succeeding issues, and identify principles and/or potential points within the group. Are the groups actions and inactions compatible with their racial goals in terms persons in the group, as stated below.

a. Mission/Vision

b. Policies

c. Procedures

d. Other institutional acts – and activism

Central persons in the institution

e. Leadership Team

f. Other staff

g. Members

h. Visitors/Guests

i. Quarterly Gathering of Leaders to Discuss Racial Issues/Plans

3. Will there be surveys/pilot methods/interviews used to gather data to enhance **feedback** about general information and deeper insights of our racist/anti-racist findings?

4. **Accountability** for making a group's continued actions more effective and sensitive

a. Quarterly Gatherings – continued and re-created by the group

b. Leadership Team

c. Group's Decision-Making Council

d. Coordination with racially focused teams

e. Other syncretic/coalition approaches

How does becoming anti-racist affect our **actions in the local and broader communities**? Small, incremental steps can be valuable locally and nationally. Consider how we can even take action against some of the most violent perpetrators of racial injury. Furthermore, institutions often do not protect themselves. Sometimes institutions are deprived of vitality, and turn into a simulacrum of what they once were, so that they can effectively gird the new order.

Take an institution you care about…and take its side. We tend to assume that institutions will automatically maintain themselves against even the most direct attacks. Many Germans made that mistake about Hitler (Snyder 22, 24). What actions can your institution take toward

   a.   Local and/or national organizations

   b.   White Nationalists/White Supremacists

   c.   Institutions working for racial justice - public, non-profit, private

Conversational Questions over Race

An intriguing lead question presents a troublesome way for beginning conversations about race. "Where are you from?" when posed by white persons may end discussions with people of color.

For people of color, that question can provoke awkward and disquieting experiences. One important insight is that the question communicates separation. An underlying assumption suggests that the respondent is not from around here. That means that they might be recent migrants, undocumented workers, persons with language differences and accents, or carrying some type of different "baggage." Also, that question can suggest that you do not belong here. All of those responses to the question are unsettling and negative while possibly overlooking the cultural backgrounds and career contributions the new person brings. At a deep level, the result of the question can cause pain. Immediate conversational hurt can be almost nothing compared to the person being a victim of torture from their home country. And the pain of the journey to arrive here can be incredible.

In a carefully sensitive situation, how can we use the "come from" question?

"Where do you come from?" is a poem from the transnational author, Dr. Meena Alexander. It has been applied to some inter-racial discussion experiences (Grose 2022). Dr. Alexander, the Indian and Sudanese scholar, shapes her poem around her early origins.

For example, the poem's title has been used to begin pursuing participants' differences and how they understand the ways in which their origins have molded their current interracial lives. Poignant responses can impact those origins that still make a difference in our lives?. Exploring that initial question from Alexander within a suitable setting can encourage understanding and mutual respect.

Questions for New Racial Encounters

1. What a pleasure that you came to this gathering!

2. Are you curious about how I decided to come to this get-together? Other sensitive questions also may occur. Consider that the following question may be a leap in the conversation.

3. Here are some reasons that I consider discussing the sensitive topic like race? How does the discussion about race work for you?

I am inspired by Dr. Ibram X Kendi's confrontations with racism. How do his ideas and mine engage some of our ongoing plans to undo racism?

He struggles for anti-racist power to make a difference. That means influencing a policymaker's decision-making. Here are some of his suggestions: "Joining an antiracist organization. Publicly donating my time with or privately donating my funds to antiracist policymakers, organizations, and protests fixated on changing power and policy" (Kendi 226).

I am challenged to make Kendi's practical thrusts a continuing part of my long-time racial passion. This means attempting to work with those in the legislative power structure. Engagements about race with friends, relatives and colleagues will challenge my patience and wisdom. My imagination is not to be fooled by my understanding of racial insights. That means seeking reality and clinging to it. My truth-seeking will be tested by my encounters with the print media, others, and my spirituality. I will unequivocally address those sensitive issues and feelings. And I relish the confidence, satisfaction and strength that results. May deeper equality be hastened, continuous, and transformative.

The idea of race, and racist acts, can be eliminated from our culture in many generations and by billions of positive acts. It was created long ago so it can be unwrapped and eliminated.

1. How do you see Kendi's views being relevant to work within state legislatures and congress?

2. In what kinds of advocacy and action groups could you engage to make a difference about racism? Research and act.

Conclusion

This entire book does not intend to be comprehensive, although it is inclusive. It is the best the author could do at this moment in 2023. It is not racial differences that are the problem. Rather, it is how we think and feel about those differences.

The readers may have other consequential initiatives to eradicate race and its damaging hierarchy. Bravo. Each active individual can decide with group coordination to change the world for social justice. Is the "unthinkable" now "thinkable"? Is the "undoable" now "doable"?

Wrap Up

May your feelings be fueled with compassion and your thoughts be ennobled by inspiration. Your deep sense of engagement with this chapter may prompt a personal change that is compelling. Change for our country's racial identity must be transformative. This means filling our future with fortitude.

Your story will be embracing the impact of unwrapping race and racial hierarchy in this chapter.

1. Journal what struck you while engaging your deeper feelings about dismantling the power of race.

2. Write your candid thoughts about new pathways to confront race.

3. Conclude your story by probing any personal change that surfaced while grappling with new, constructive approaches to each day's experience.

What Types of **Questions** May Still be Needed to Dig into **Racial Reality?**

1. EXPLORATORY - What comes to mind when you think about race? What else do we need to know about this issue?

2. BELIEFS - How is our belief system relevant to oppressors and the oppressed?

3. POWER - How do we address power, privilege and difference in our relationships?

4. UNDERSTANDING - What difference does race make in understanding human interactions?

5. SPECIFIC CHOICE - In discussions about race, which racial expressions offer the greatest viability: white supremacy, race relations, racial differences, human differences, or other terms?

6. ESSENTIAL - What is key to expressing your story about race?

7. OPINION - What advice do you have in dealing with race relations?

8. CHANGE - Under what conditions or circumstances would we expect major adjustments to be made in race relations? In what ways are we open to change personally and institutionally to enhance social justice?

9. CRITICAL THINKING - Looking deeply at racial problem-solving, how do we contrast different issues?

10. EVALUATION - What are the markers for racial progress in our individual lives and our institutions?

Works Cited

Alexander, Meena. "Where do You Come From?" New York, 2018.

Grose, Charles. Information from the Racial Advisory Team at Mayflower UCC, Minneapolis, 2022.

Hackman Consulting. Adapted from Beverly Tatum in "Defining Racism: 'Can We talk?'" in READINGS FOR DIVERSITY AND SOCIAL JUSTICE, 2000.

Kendi, Abram X. HOW TO BE AN ANTI-RACIST? One World, 2019, p. 226.

McGhee, Heather. THE SUM OF US. One World, 2021, pp. 282-289.

Minutes of the Board of Regents of The University of Texas System. Vol 1, 12 Sep. 1969.

Snyder, Timothy. ON TYRANY. Tim Duggan Books, 2017, pp. 22, 24.

West, Cornel. RACE MATTERS. Vintage Books, 1993, p. 156.

Index

www.ingramcontent.com/pod-product-compliance
Lightning Source LLC
Chambersburg PA
CBHW062038270326
41929CB00014B/2471